OUR
WORK
IS
EVERYWHERE

# OUR WORK IS EVERYWHERE

## AN ILLUSTRATED ORAL HISTORY OF QUEER & TRANS RESISTANCE

### SYAN ROSE

ARSENAL PULP PRESS

xʷməθkʷəy̓əm (MUSQUEAM), Sḵwx̱wú7mesh (SQUAMISH), and

səl̓ilwəta ʔɬ (TSLEIL-WAUTUTH) LAND

(VANCOUVER)

**OUR WORK IS EVERYWHERE**

SECOND PRINTING: 2021

ARSENAL PULP PRESS
Suite 202 – 211 East Georgia St.
Vancouver, BC V6A 1Z6
Canada
*arsenalpulp.com*

Arsenal Pulp Press acknowledges the xʷməθkʷəy̓əm (Musqueam), Sḵwx̱wú7mesh (Squamish), and səl̓ilwəta?ł (Tsleil-Waututh) Nations, custodians of the traditional, ancestral, and unceded territories where our office is located. We pay respect to their histories, traditions, and continuous living cultures and commit to accountability, respectful relations, and friendship.

"Reclaiming & Revolting Bodies: *Fat: The Play*" originally appeared in *Truthout*, March 21, 2016.
"We Are All Elders," a collaborative comic with Vivi Veronica, originally appeared in *Bitch*, 2018.

Cover art by Syan Rose
Layout support by Jazmin Welch
Proofread by Alison Strobel

Printed and bound in Canada

Library and Archives Canada Cataloguing in Publication:
Title: Our work is everywhere : an illustrated oral history of queer and trans resistance / Syan Rose.
Names: Rose, Syan, 1990– author, artist.
Identifiers: Canadiana (print) 20200211188 | Canadiana (ebook) 20200211277 |
  ISBN 9781551528151 (softcover) | ISBN 9781551528168 (HTML)
Subjects: LCSH: Gays—Political activity—Comic books, strips, etc. | LCSH: Sexual minorities—
  Political activity—Comic books, strips, etc. | LCSH: Transgender people—Political activity—
  Comic books, strips, etc. | LCSH: Gender-nonconforming people—Political activity—
  Comic books, strips, etc. | LCSH: Gay rights—Comic books, strips, etc. | LCSH: Political activists—
  Comic books, strips, etc. | LCGFT: Nonfiction comics.
Classification: LCC HQ76.5 .R67 2021 | DDC 323.3/26022—dc23

# CONTENTS

# FOREWORD

OUR WORK IS OUR QUEER SURVIVAL HUSTLE BEAUTY BLOOM
OUR WORK IS LOVE

---

All the times people have said, *you're so busy, you're so productive, wow I wish I could do what you do, you must be really slammed, wow I know, life is crazy, right?*

All the times people have said, *flaky, irresponsible, do you even have a job? we wanted reliable, you've canceled a lot, unfortunately we don't offer sick leave, you're still crying? oh, you're "suddenly sick" and can't make it? oooookay. working from home is only allowed under very limited circumstances and must be requested and approved in advance, you'll want to bring your proof of disability, i'm sorry, your work didn't show signs of consistent excellence, so you didn't receive the fellowship.*

All the times I have: spent time repotting the geranium that hangs at my front door. Faffed about, walking around in my sleep shirt and some booty shorts, picking up things, putting the kettle on, answering a text—and then getting an Idea. And sitting down, in that same messy house, in those same stanky booty shorts, and wrote about it, ignoring my phone.

All the times I had a twenty-hour-a-week (at least) unpaid job listening, giving resources, cracking jokes, driving someone to the clinic, bringing tacos. And sometimes, receiving same.

All the times I worked and worked and worked, up 'til 2 AM on some project I'd get a hundred dollars for, sending emails 'til my eyes burned, wakingup and going to openthestore, getpickedupbymybosstoteachmedstudents-thepelvic, teachthewebinar, dotheaccessrun-through, catchtheplaneontimetogospeakat-thecollege, and—collapseandrecover afterwards.

our work
this work
this queer work
this queer everyday labor
everywhere
every where
everywhere?

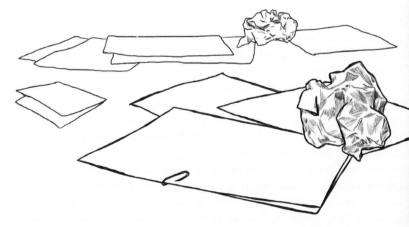

the labor of being depressed and Black and
female
the labor of writing
and producing
and directing
a Fat queer play
in Texas
the labor of making
a queer Brown healing collective
in Flatbush
the work
of being a Black woman
in pain,
emotional and physical
keeping a roof over your head
sitting in your room
typing your stories
as the rain falls on the roof
and feeling your way
through legacy
of what it means to be Black, female, raised
poor
and writing
"sometimes I feel embarrassed & foolish
to think that I should be a writer,
a working writer.

who the fuck am I, the daughter of two people
who didn't even finish middle school, to think
that I can do all these things that my mother
couldn't?" (Raven Taylor)

or when Dusty LaMay says,
"I know you want me to talk about astrology
or legal work ...
Both are vehicles through which I hope these
greater skills are channeling to my community:
self-forgiveness,
boundary appreciation,
self-actualization, & self-determination."

is that work?
that is work.
this is work.
our work is everywhere
even as it's
shitted on, despised, and erased.
it's still here, speaking.

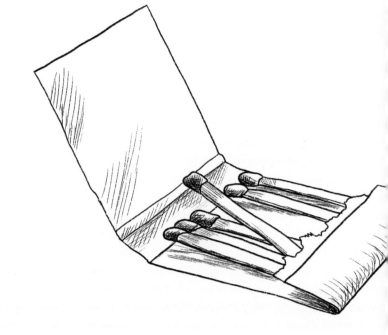

Reading and witnessing
this gorgeous graphic novel storykeeping book,
what echoed in me was how much I live with an
everyday reverberation
that none of the work i do is real
that none of the work i do matters
that all of the labor I pour like stars
into this world
is illegitimate
laughable
the way that one white woman once laughed,
"oh you don't need a contract, you're just doing
a little job, it's not real work."

But i know I wake up from a disabled sleep and
work
getting to go make the tea and the coffee is
work
texting three friends asking them how they are,
work
answering emails
lying curled on a couch crying and mourning
getting myself to the clinic
coordinating a complicated transformative
justice process—aren't they all—that has taken
hundreds of hours and years,
writing poems
and stories
and editing an essay
and writing this foreword
and sweeping the floor
and following up
and harvesting herbs
and folding the laundry
and caring
and giving a shit
and caring—
an endless river
of care
presence
and brilliance
and tiredness
and brilliant tiredness—
but there
always there
is all
Work
Our work

9

Because work is not the problem. Our souls glow and grow from wanting to create, heal, scheme. Capitalism is the problem. Racism is the problem. Ableism is the problem. All we do to keep ourselves and our kin here is not the problem.

As Vivi Veronica says:
"Trans women survive, love, & exist because of the knowledge we pass down. She's my sister. She's dead & alive. She's my auntie. My mother. Me ... All the trans-feminine bodies & spirits I've known continue to teach me. Not all of my sisters are still alive, but their wisdom impacts the footsteps of those still here ... One day I decided my body was not a tragedy. On that day I knew I would live forever."

parenting Lebanese and queer in diaspora
making "trials" and stating in all caps
EVERYTHING YOU LOVE ABOUT NEW
ORLEANS IS BECAUSE OF BLACK PEOPLE
reading the encyclopedia
surviving living trans in prison for a decade

we
who are called lazy
and shiftless
and what do you do all day anyway?
we whose lives' work is laughed at and
dismissed
crumbs brushed off a table

"But still, someone, something, needs to hold us" (Ra Malika Imhotep)
and we do.

These story pictures hold us. Reflect us. Ensure we will not be forgotten. Reflect our beauty and our sweat. Give us stories that may help us remember:
our shit is really, really real.

These stories are a queerly beautiful labor. Sarah/Syan has written and drawn our lives in their exact specific queer crip BIPOC sex worker gorgeousness. Into history, so they'll never be forgotten. And so they can be a seed library passed around that kin near and far—including kin we may never meet—can plant from. Her queerfemmeChineseJewishWhite art care work as an artist is a labor of queer love.

---

*with love and labor*
*and so much appreciation for the work of this book,*
**LEAH LAKSHMI PIEPZNA-SAMARASINHA**
SEPTEMBER 1, 2020

# OUR WORK IS EVERYWHERE

IS AN ANTHOLOGY OF ILLUSTRATED INTERVIEWS WITH & WRITINGS BY QUEER & TRANS ORGANIZERS, HEALERS, ARTISTS, & COMRADES. IT'S PART GRAPHIC NONFICTION, PART THANK-YOU NOTE, PART GAY THEORY PAPER, PART ACTIVIST GOSSIP COLUMN, & THE REST IS A SURREALIST DREAM IN WHICH WE KNOW WHY WE'RE HERE & WHAT WE NEED TO DO. THE VOICES IN THIS BOOK SPEAK & WRITE CANDIDLY ABOUT THEIR EXPERIENCES OF OPPRESSION, PAIN, NONPROFITS, POP CULTURE, THE CRIMINAL INJUSTICE SYSTEM & LOVE TO CREATE A NUANCED LANDSCAPE WHERE NEW & PROGRESSIVE WORLD'S ARE IMAGINED. THESE CONVERSATIONS HAVE HELPED ME UNDERSTAND MORE ABOUT HOW TO SHIFT POWER ON AN INSTITUTIONAL & INTERPERSONAL LEVEL, & WITHIN MYSELF.

WORKING ON THESE DRAWINGS HAS BEEN A CATHARTIC PROCESS FOR ME. AS AN ANXIOUS PERSON, MY DRAWING TIME HAS BECOME A SACRED SITE FOR SAVORING SILENCE & ALONE-NESS & CHANNELING TENSE ENERGY INTO FOCUS. IT'S BEEN A CHALLENGE TO USE MY ILLUSTRATION SKILLS THOUGHTFULLY & INTENTIONALLY TO EXAMINE POLITICS, RELATIONSHIPS, & IDENTITY ESPECIALLY IN A TIME THAT VALUES MEDIA THAT CAN BE CREATED & FORGOTTEN WITHIN MINUTES. DURING INSECURE MOMENTS, I'VE WONDERED IF THIS PROJECT HAS TAKEN TOO LONG (FIVE YEARS) TO BE RELEVANT. BUT THAT TYPE OF THINKING IS ROOTED IN A PERFECTIONIST, HYPER-PRODUCTIVE IDEOLOGY.

ARTISTS NEED TO WORK AT THE PACE THAT'S RIGHT FOR THEM.

I STARTED RECORDING THESE CONVERSATIONS IN 2015, WHEN I LIVED ON DUWAMISH LAND (SEATTLE), & MY LIFE AS AN OUT QUEER PERSON BROUGHT ME FACE-TO-FACE WITH COMPLICATED QUESTIONS ABOUT POWER, DESIRE, JUSTICE, & ACCOUNTABILITY. I WITNESSED QUEER & TRANS FRIENDS, LOVES, & ACQUAINTANCES ACROSS RACE & CLASS LINES TRYING THEIR BEST TO FORM ALTERNATIVES TO THE VIOLENCE OF OUR SOCIETY BY REDISTRIBUTING WEALTH, SHIFTING CONVERSATIONS ABOUT "DESIRABLE" BODIES, PAYING REPARATIONS TO BLACK & INDIGENOUS PEOPLE, LEARNING ABOUT & SUPPORTING ONE ANOTHER'S ACCESS NEEDS, & TRYING TO HEAL FROM RACIALIZED & ANCESTRAL TRAUMA.

WHEN I SAY, "OUR WORK IS EVERYWHERE," I INTEND TO EXPAND THE DEFINITION OF "WORK" BEYOND WHAT IS RECOGNIZABLE & CONSIDERED VALUABLE UNDER CAPITALISM; INSTEAD, I CLAIM THAT THE WORK THAT'S NEEDED TO REALLY CHANGE OUR WORLD IS THE OPPOSITE OF WHAT MOST OF US GET A PAYCHECK FOR: IT'S THE EMOTIONAL SUPPORT WE GIVE TO OTHERS, IT'S THE MEALS WE COOK FOR EACH OTHER, IT'S THE BRILLIANT IDEAS WE HAVE, THE JOKES WE TELL, THE HARD CONVERSATIONS WE ENGAGE IN WITH OURSELVES & OTHERS. ALL OF THAT CHAOTIC, UNDEFINED, EVER-CHANGING WORK DESERVES CREDIT, TOO. AND THAT'S WHAT I'VE TRIED TO DO HERE: GIVE CREDIT TO JUST A FEW OF THE MANY PEOPLE WHO HAVE PUT IN THE WORK TO CHIP AWAY AT THE STRUCTURAL & MENTAL RACISM, TRANSPHOBIA, FATPHOBIA, COLONIALISM, ABLEISM, XENOPHOBIA, ANTI-BLACKNESS, RAPE CULTURE, & OTHER HARMFUL SYSTEMS WE HAVE ALL GROWN UP IN &, UNFORTUNATELY, BEEN PART OF REPRODUCING TO VARYING DEGREES.

THROUGH INTIMACY WITH QUEER & TRANS PEOPLE, I REALIZED I HAD (& STILL HAVE) SO MUCH WORK TO DO AROUND UNLEARNING THE TOXIC BELIEFS & VALUES SOCIETY HAD INSTILLED IN ME. WITNESSING THE WORK QUEER & TRANS PEOPLE WERE DOING HELPED ME DEVELOP MY OWN ROAD MAP TO NAVIGATE THESE COMPLICATED ISSUES & RELATIONSHIPS.

MUCH OF THIS WORK HAS BEEN MESSY, HEARTBREAKING, & CONFUSING. I STILL STRUGGLE WITH PERFECTIONISM & SELF-FORGIVENESS. I STILL FEEL LET DOWN BY THE MYTHICAL "QUEER COMMUNITY," BUT WORKING ON THIS PROJECT & LEARNING FROM SUCH INSIGHTFUL & CREATIVE PEOPLE HAS CONTIN-UALLY REMINDED ME THAT EVERY SINGLE ONE OF US HAS OUR OWN PATH TO BUILDING SOMETHING NEW.

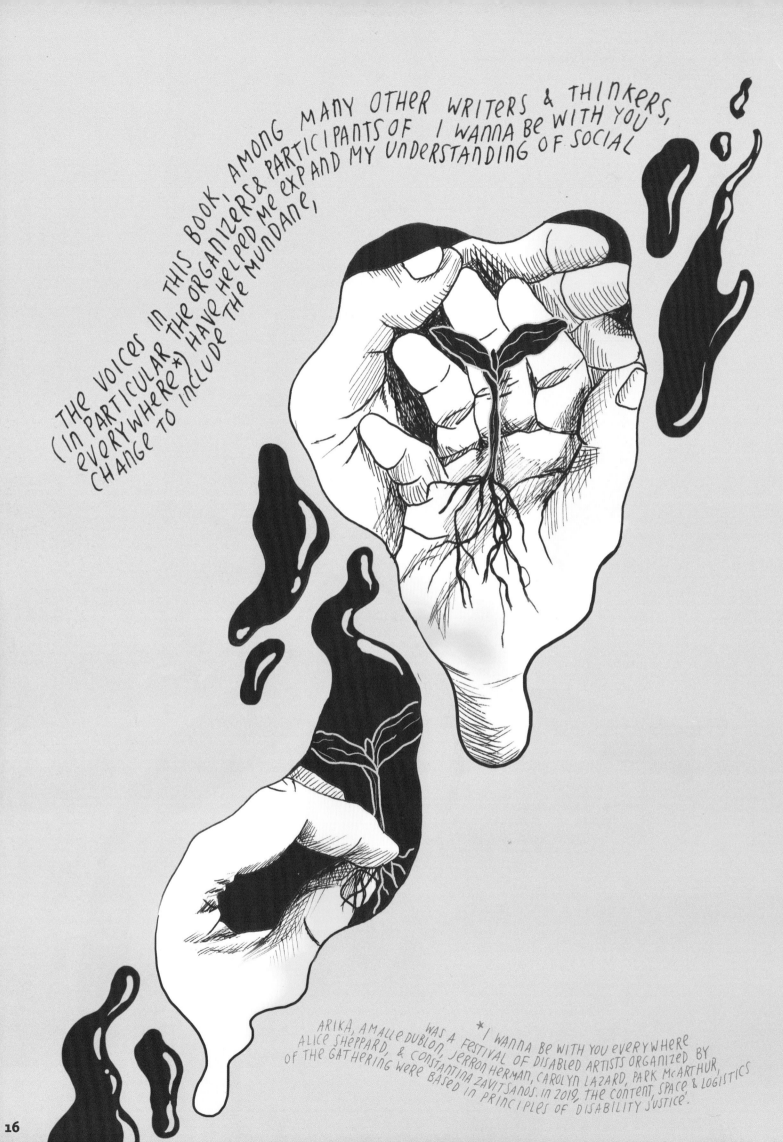

THE VOICES IN THIS BOOK, AMONG MANY OTHER WRITERS & THINKERS, (IN PARTICULAR THE ORGANIZERS & PARTICIPANTS OF I WANNA BE WITH YOU EVERYWHERE*) HAVE HELPED ME EXPAND MY UNDERSTANDING OF SOCIAL CHANGE TO INCLUDE THE MUNDANE,

*I WANNA BE WITH YOU EVERYWHERE WAS A FESTIVAL OF DISABLED ARTISTS ORGANIZED BY ARIKA, AMALLE DUBLON, ALICE SHEPPARD, JERRON HERMAN, CAROLYN LAZARD, PARK McARTHUR, & CONSTANTINA ZAVITSANOS. IN 2019, THE CONTENT, SPACE, & LOGISTICS OF THE GATHERING WERE BASED IN PRINCIPLES OF 'DISABILITY JUSTICE'.

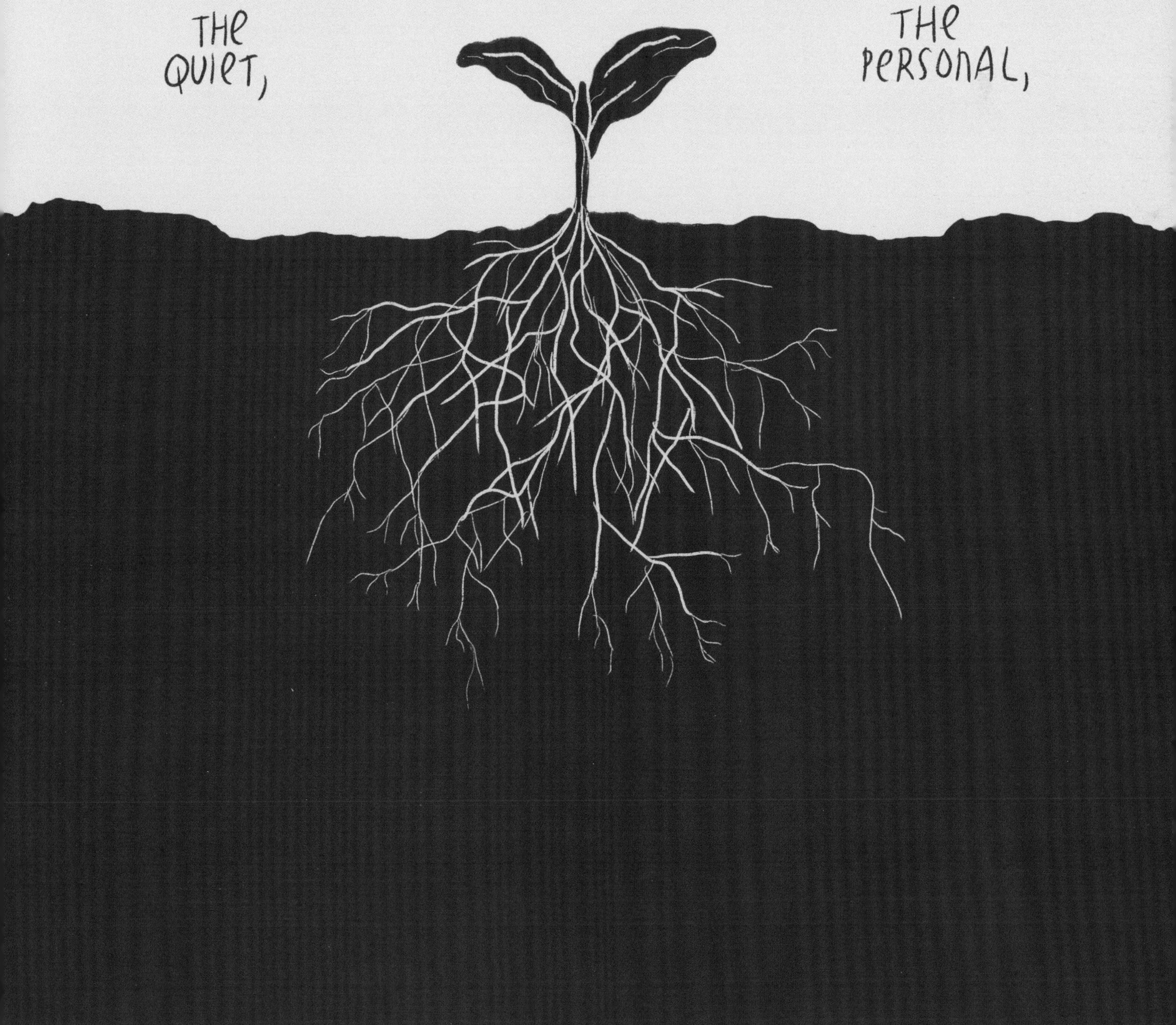
the quiet,
the personal,

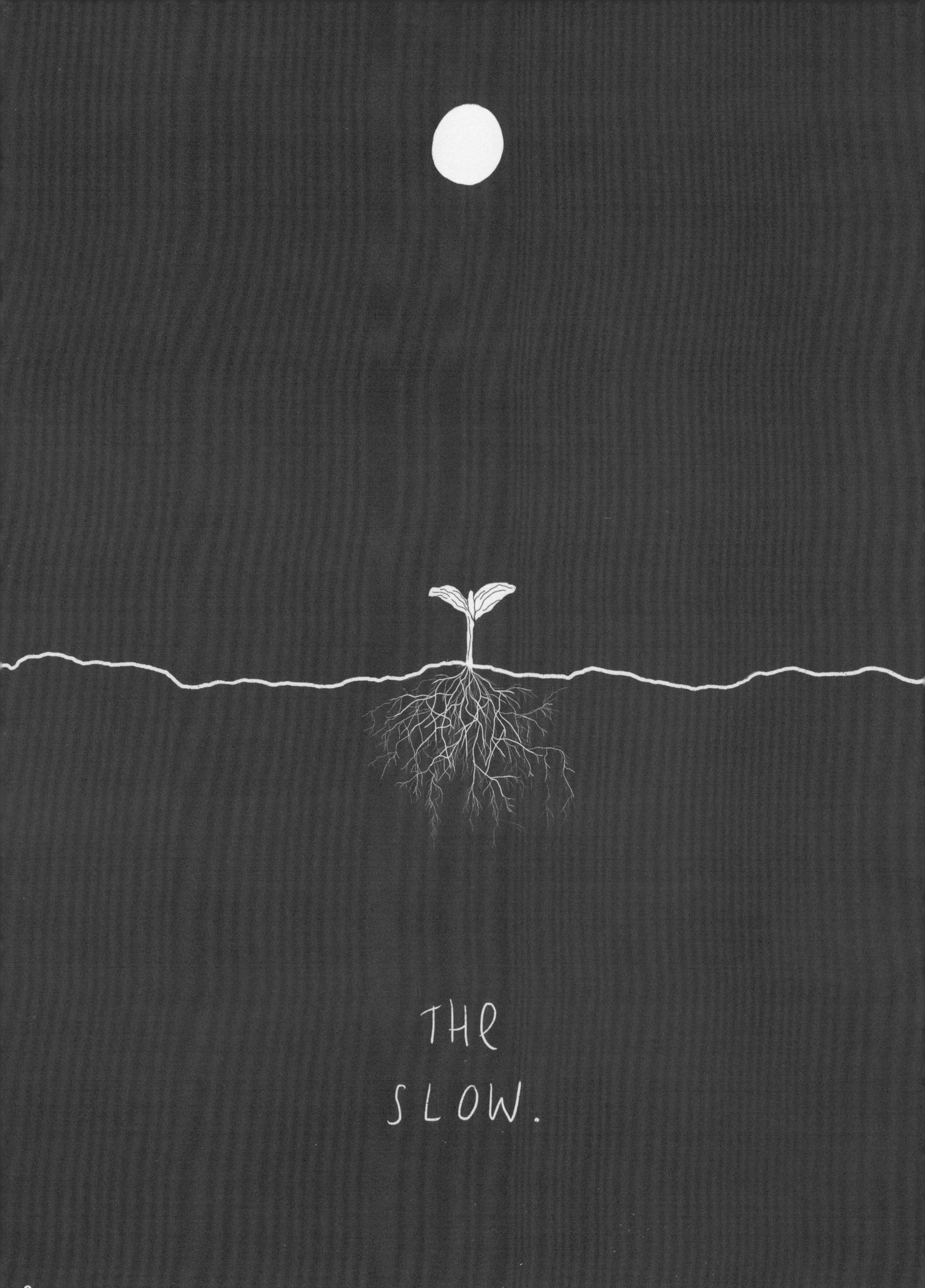
THE
SLOW.

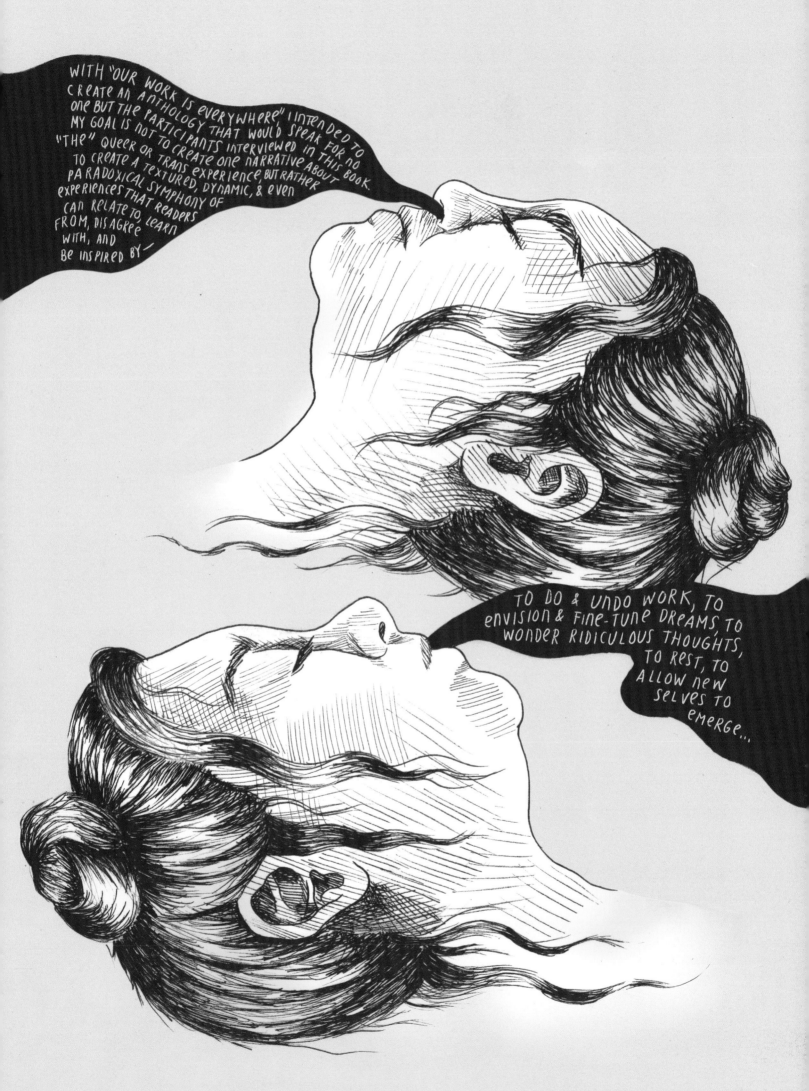

WITH "OUR WORK IS EVERYWHERE" I INTENDED TO CREATE AN ANTHOLOGY THAT WOULD SPEAK FOR NO ONE BUT THE PARTICIPANTS INTERVIEWED IN THIS BOOK. MY GOAL IS NOT TO CREATE ONE NARRATIVE ABOUT "THE" QUEER OR TRANS EXPERIENCE, BUT RATHER TO CREATE A TEXTURED, DYNAMIC, & EVEN PARADOXICAL SYMPHONY OF EXPERIENCES THAT READERS CAN RELATE TO, LEARN FROM, DISAGREE WITH, AND BE INSPIRED BY—

TO DO & UNDO WORK, TO ENVISION & FINE-TUNE DREAMS TO WONDER RIDICULOUS THOUGHTS, TO REST, TO ALLOW NEW SELVES TO EMERGE...

# CRYING CUZ THE WIND BLEW

A CONVERSATION WITH RAVEN TAYLOR

Two years ago, I was struggling with homelessness, which happened because I got really sick mentally & was going through a deep bout of depression so I quit all my jobs & just couch surfed.

Now I'm out of that, but it's still so hard for me because I have to maintain a roof over my head, feed myself, & pay my bills. & the more I go to work, the more I feel depressed & tired & unmotivated so then I don't make art. & then dealing with chronic pain & mental illness, every time I have to quit a job or call out of work & don't have "proof" of what's wrong with me,

It's like I'm not living up to the standards of productivity or what it means to be an adult.

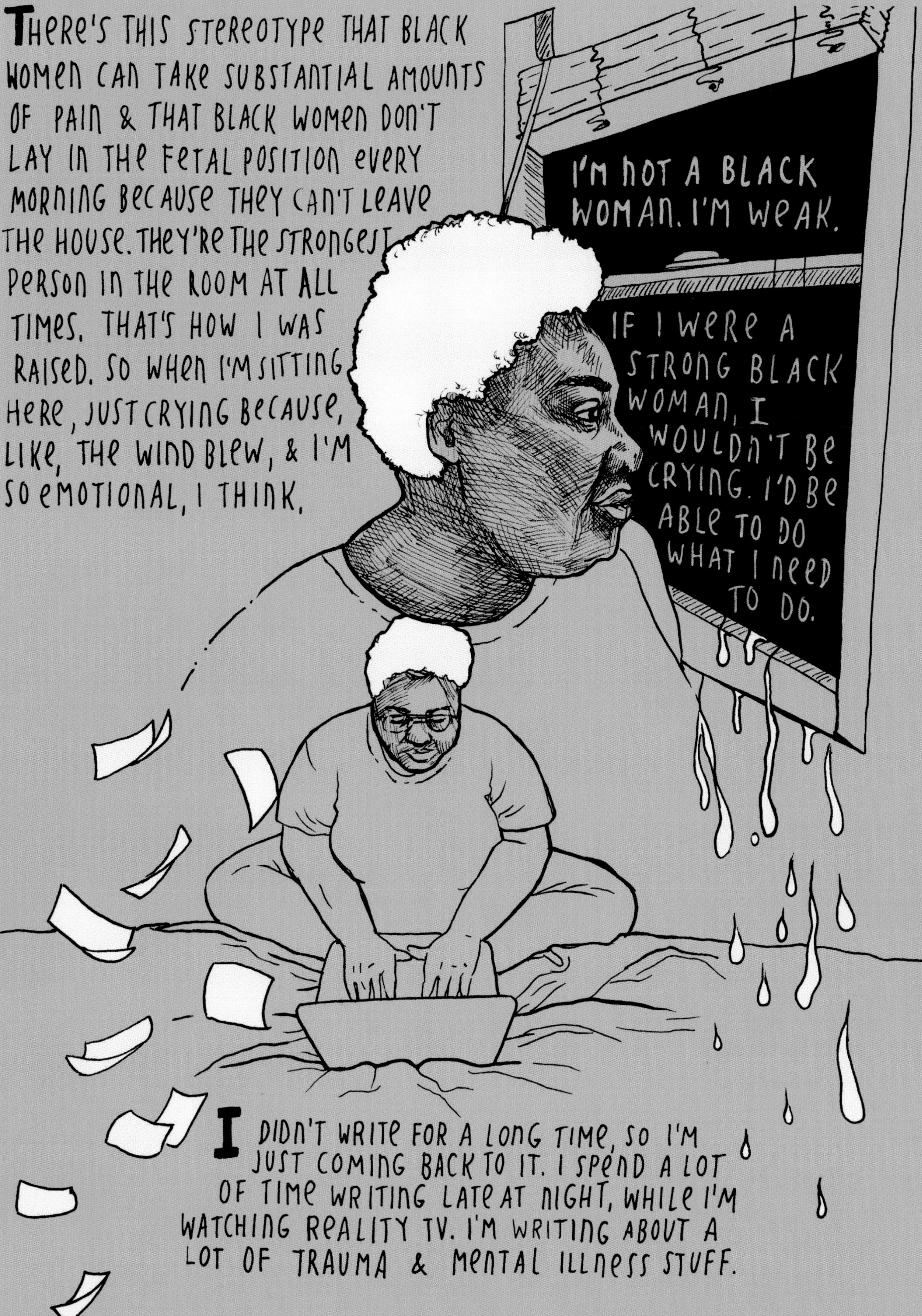
THERE'S THIS STEREOTYPE THAT BLACK WOMEN CAN TAKE SUBSTANTIAL AMOUNTS OF PAIN & THAT BLACK WOMEN DON'T LAY IN THE FETAL POSITION EVERY MORNING BECAUSE THEY CAN'T LEAVE THE HOUSE. THEY'RE THE STRONGEST PERSON IN THE ROOM AT ALL TIMES. THAT'S HOW I WAS RAISED. SO WHEN I'M SITTING HERE, JUST CRYING BECAUSE, LIKE, THE WIND BLEW, & I'M SO EMOTIONAL, I THINK,
I'M NOT A BLACK WOMAN. I'M WEAK.
IF I WERE A STRONG BLACK WOMAN, I WOULDN'T BE CRYING. I'D BE ABLE TO DO WHAT I NEED TO DO.
I DIDN'T WRITE FOR A LONG TIME, SO I'M JUST COMING BACK TO IT. I SPEND A LOT OF TIME WRITING LATE AT NIGHT, WHILE I'M WATCHING REALITY TV. I'M WRITING ABOUT A LOT OF TRAUMA & MENTAL ILLNESS STUFF.

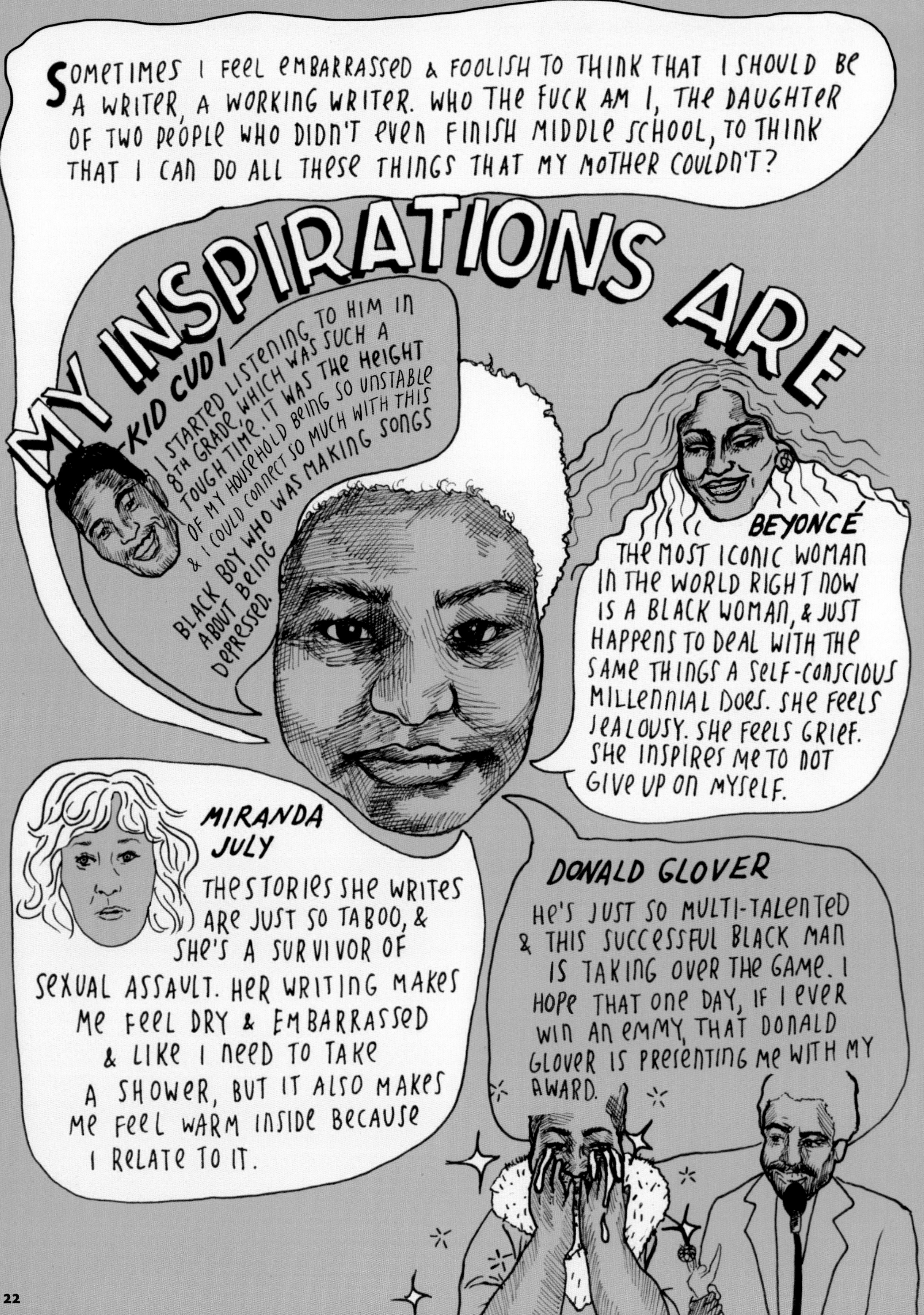
SOMETIMES I FEEL EMBARRASSED & FOOLISH TO THINK THAT I SHOULD BE A WRITER, A WORKING WRITER. WHO THE FUCK AM I, THE DAUGHTER OF TWO PEOPLE WHO DIDN'T EVEN FINISH MIDDLE SCHOOL, TO THINK THAT I CAN DO ALL THESE THINGS THAT MY MOTHER COULDN'T?
MY INSPIRATIONS ARE
KID CUDI
I STARTED LISTENING TO HIM IN 8TH GRADE, WHICH WAS SUCH A TOUGH TIME. IT WAS THE HEIGHT OF MY HOUSEHOLD BEING SO UNSTABLE & I COULD CONNECT SO MUCH WITH THIS BLACK BOY WHO WAS MAKING SONGS ABOUT BEING DEPRESSED.
BEYONCÉ
THE MOST ICONIC WOMAN IN THE WORLD RIGHT NOW IS A BLACK WOMAN, & JUST HAPPENS TO DEAL WITH THE SAME THINGS A SELF-CONSCIOUS MILLENNIAL DOES. SHE FEELS JEALOUSY. SHE FEELS GRIEF. SHE INSPIRES ME TO NOT GIVE UP ON MYSELF.
MIRANDA JULY
THE STORIES SHE WRITES ARE JUST SO TABOO, & SHE'S A SURVIVOR OF SEXUAL ASSAULT. HER WRITING MAKES ME FEEL DRY & EMBARRASSED & LIKE I NEED TO TAKE A SHOWER, BUT IT ALSO MAKES ME FEEL WARM INSIDE BECAUSE I RELATE TO IT.
DONALD GLOVER
HE'S JUST SO MULTI-TALENTED & THIS SUCCESSFUL BLACK MAN IS TAKING OVER THE GAME. I HOPE THAT ONE DAY, IF I EVER WIN AN EMMY, THAT DONALD GLOVER IS PRESENTING ME WITH MY AWARD.

# OUR OWN DIVINITY

## A CONVERSATION WITH DUSTY LAMAY

WHAT SKILLS DO YOU PERSONALLY BRING TO YOUR COMMUNITY?

I KNOW YOU WANT ME TO TALK ABOUT ASTROLOGY OR LEGAL WORK BUT I DON'T KNOW IF THAT IS HOW I WOULD ANSWER FIRST! BOTH ARE VEHICLES THROUGH WHICH I HOPE THESE GREATER SKILLS ARE CHANNELING TO MY COMMUNITY: SELF-FORGIVENESS, BOUNDARY APPRECIATION, SELF-ACTUALIZATION, & SELF-DETERMINATION TO HELP ACHIEVE COMMUNAL CONSIOUSNESS RAISING.

AS QUEERS, WE HAVE BEEN SOCIALLY DIVORCED FROM GOD & HOLINESS. AT LEAST IN JUDEO-CHRISTIAN AMERICA, MANY OF US WERE RAISED BEING TAUGHT THAT WHO WE ARE IS INHERENTLY SINFUL, AN ABOMINATION, UNHOLY.

*ARIES*

ASTROLOGY IS AN AVENUE THROUGH WHICH QUEERS CAN ACCESS OUR OWN SPIRITUAL WORTH & CONNECT TO OUR OWN DIVINITY VOID OF THE TRAUMA OF CHRISTIAN SOCIALIZATION & JUDGMENT.

*VIRGO*

SUPRISINGLY, THERE ARE A LOT OF SIMILARITIES BETWEEN MY JOBS AS AN ASTROLOGER & A LEGAL ADVOCATE. IN BOTH OF THESE ROLES I CAN HAVE IMMENSE POWER OVER A PERSON'S LIFE & I TRY TO REMAIN AWARE AT ALL TIMES OF THAT POTENTIAL IMBALANCE OF POWER.

IN MY EXPERIENCE, IN POWER-DIFFERENT RELATIONSHIPS PERSONALLY OR PROFESSIONALLY, IT IS BEST TO BE CLEAR & DIRECT ABOUT THE POWER IMBALANCE. TOXIC POWER CYCLES THRIVE IN INVISIBILITY.

WE MUST DRAW LIGHT TO THE TOXIC IMBALANCES IN ORDER TO HELP ADDRESS THEM & ILLUMINATE NEW WAYS OF BEING. THE SKILLS I HAVE LEARNED AS A SURVIVOR HELP IMMENSELY IN UNPACKING THE REDISTRIBUTION OF POWER. EVEN REDISTRIBUTING RESOURCES CAN BE PROBLEMATIC IF IT COMES FROM A PATERNALISTIC PLACE.

LIBRA

SOMETIMES IT IS THE PEOPLE MOST LIKE YOU WHO HAVE THE MOST POWER TO VALIDATE YOU & MAKE YOU FEEL SEEN.

GEMINI

I FEEL THIS WAY WITH MY BOYFRIEND (WHO IS NONBINARY) OR WHEN I AM WITH OTHER SIMILARLY SITUATED MIXED RACE FOLKS OR FOLKS RAISED IN OKLAHOMA

LEGAL WORK & ASTROLOGY ARE ALSO BOTH TOOLS TO HELP FIGHT ISOLATION. I ATTEMPT TO SUPPORT OTHERS IN CONNECTING BETTER TO THEIR LEGAL RIGHTS ON A PERSONAL LEVEL, OR THEIR COSMIC POTENTIAL ON A COMMUNAL LEVEL.

THIS QUEER YOUTH GROUP I WAS A PART OF AS A TEEN USED TO HELP OUT IN AIDS CARE HOUSES LOCALLY. I REMEMBER ONE VIBRANT QUEEN IN PARTICULAR TEACHING US ABOUT HOW SHE WAS ONE OF THE GO-GO GIRL BOYS THROWING HER HEELS AT THE COPS DURING THE STONEWALL RIOTS.

TOPPLING THE SYSTEMS THAT BE WILL BE DIRTY, HARD, GUT WRENCHING, SWEATY WORK THAT WILL START WITH THOSE OF US WHO ARE THE MOST OFTEN INVISIBILIZED SCREAMING THE LOUDEST & THROWING OUR HEELS & FISTS THE HARDEST AS THE WALLS OF THE PAST COME CRUMBLING DOWN TO REVEAL A DIFFERENT TOMORROW.

# RECLAIMING & REVOLTING BODIES:
## FAT: THE PLAY

In the fall of 2013, a collective of self-identified fat, queer, femme performers, writers, & community members in Austin, Texas, came together to vision, heal, & create. Out came "FAT: THE PLAY", a performance piece that shares collective members' experiences with body oppression, racism, classism, & misogyny.

The powerful, intersectional, & ever-evolving work of PLUMP continues to confront systemic & interpersonal fat-hatred by centering the narratives of those who it impacts most.

"FAT: THE PLAY" works simultaneously as a call to action for other fat queer femmes, an educational tool of activism for those with privileged bodies, & a guideline for all of us to work to unlearn our internalized prejudice against fat bodies.

### Caleb Luna
PLUMP COLLECTIVE MEMBER

ORIGINALLY WRITTEN & PERFORMED FOR THE FRONTERAFEST IN AUSTIN, A ONE-ACT FRINGE THEATER COMPETITION WHERE IT WON BEST OF THE FEST 2014, WE HAVE SINCE EXPANDED THE PLAY & PERFORMED IT TWICE MORE FOR OUR COMMUNITY. BOTH OF THESE PERFORMANCES INCLUDED ASL INTERPRETERS FOR DEAF/HARD-OF-HEARING COMMUNITY MEMBERS & A SLIDING SCALE PAYMENT SYSTEM, INITIATIVES TAKEN TO ALLOW THE BROADEST ACCESS POSSIBLE. IN JULY 2015, WE FILMED AN EXTENDED VERSION TITLED "FAT: THE FILM," ATTEMPTING TO MAKE THE PIECE AVAILABLE TO PEOPLE OUTSIDE OF AUSTIN & ACROSS THE GLOBE; IT IS CURRENTLY IN POST-PRODUCTION.

WE BEGIN THE PLAY BY CONTEXTUALIZING OUR WORK IN EVERY-DAY MESSAGES OF FAT HATRED, AND THEN DISCUSS A JOURNEY OF BEING AFRAID OF THE WORD "**FAT**" TO RECLAIMING IT.

WE TALK ABOUT, AMONG OTHER THINGS, OUR RELATIONSHIPS TO OUR BODIES, OUR CHILDHOOD EXPERIENCES, OUR GENDERS, FEMME AS A POLITICAL IDENTITY, SEX & DATING, FOOD, MENTAL ILLNESS, & OUR VARIOUS RACIAL IDENTITIES.

DIET magazine

HOW TO LOSE 20 POUNDS IN FIVE MINUTES

KALE! KALE! KALE!

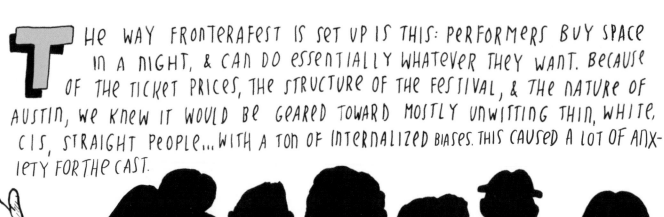

**T**HE WAY FRONTERAFEST IS SET UP IS THIS: PERFORMERS BUY SPACE IN A NIGHT, & CAN DO ESSENTIALLY WHATEVER THEY WANT. BECAUSE OF THE TICKET PRICES, THE STRUCTURE OF THE FESTIVAL, & THE NATURE OF AUSTIN, WE KNEW IT WOULD BE GEARED TOWARD MOSTLY UNWITTING THIN, WHITE, CIS, STRAIGHT PEOPLE...WITH A TON OF INTERNALIZED BIASES. THIS CAUSED A LOT OF ANXIETY FOR THE CAST.

PICTURED: LEMONS CLEMONS

OUR INITIAL PERFORMANCE WAS ACTUALLY AMAZING BECAUSE OUR COMMUNITY PACKED THE HOUSE.

IT FELT SO GOOD TO HAVE THE SUPPORT OF ALL OUR FRIENDS... WE WERE MET WITH THUNDEROUS CHEERS & APPLAUSE. WE WEREN'T EXPECTING TO ADVANCE IN THE COMPETITION, BUT WE DID.

OUR SECOND PERFORMANCE, AT THE BEST OF THE WEEK, WAS ROUGH...FOR THE MOST PART THE AUDIENCE WAS FILLED WITH STRANGERS & THEY WERE DOWNRIGHT HOSTILE. THEY WERE REALLY UNRESPONSIVE & ICY TO OUR MESSAGES, & LAUGHED AT THE PARTS THAT WERE NOT JOKES. IT LEFT US FEELING REALLY DOWNTRODDEN & DEFEATED. AND THEN, TO EVERYONE'S SUPRISE, WE MADE IT TO THE BEST OF THE FEST.

# FAT ACTIVISM LOOKS A LOT OF DIFFERENT WAYS.

MY PRIMARY INTRODUCTION TO FAT ACTIVISM WAS THROUGH BLOGGING & SITES LIKE TUMBLR. "FAT: THE PLAY" & PLUMP WAS THE REALLY BUILT IN-PERSON COMMUNITY WITH AN INTENT- IONAL WAY, & IT FIRST TIME I HAD EVER OTHER FAT PEOPLE IN WAS REALLY BEAUT- IFUL & HEALING.

WHAT I HAD PRIMARILY CONSIDERED MY ACTIVISM PREVIOUSLY WAS DAILY VISIBILITY.

BUT THERE ARE BOOKS WRITTEN ABOUT FAT- NESS; IT IS AN ENTIRE ACADEMIC FIELD OF STUDY, PROTESTS, DANCES, ETC. I IMAGINE "FAT: THE PLAY" TO EVEN BE IN A LINEAGE OF FAT PERFORMANCE ART AFTER THE STAGE PLAY "THE PANZA MONOLOGUES."

I'VE NEVER EXPERIENCED ANYTHING LIKE "FAT: THE PLAY." IN THE BEGINNING, I WAS JUST SO THRILLED TO BE A PART OF SOMETHING THAT WAS BY & FOR FAT FEMMES. OUR STORIES ARE SO OFTEN ERASED IN QUEER STORIES & HISTORIES THAT IT FELT REALLY POWERFUL TO SIT IN A CIRCLE, TO SHARE FOOD, & TO TALK ABOUT THE JOY, STRUGGLE, & COMPLEXITIES OF BEING A FAT, QUEER FEMME OF COLOR.

nicole arteaga PLUMP COLLECTIVE MEMBER

I GOT INVOLVED NOT BECAUSE I WAS ACTUALLY WANTING TO MAKE ART OR PERFORM IN A PLAY, BUT BECAUSE I WAS REALLY CRAVING FAT QUEER COMMUNITY... AND ALTHOUGH I WAS ALREADY DOING A LOT OF WORK TO UNLEARN MY OWN INTERNALIZED FAT-HATRED & SELF-LOATHING, I WAS TIRED & IT WAS HARD.

AS WE CONTINUED TO MEET & WRITE & THIS PLAY BEGAN TO TAKE SHAPE, I HAD TO REALLY CHALLENGE MYSELF TO BE VULNERABLE & OPEN ABOUT SOME OF THE MOST TRAUMATIC, PAINFUL PARTS OF MYSELF... IT WAS NEARLY IMPOSSIBLE TO GET PAST MY FEELINGS OF INADEQUACY & LACK OF SELF-WORTH, BUT ALL THE FEMMES WERE SUPER AFFIRMING & VALIDATING.

TO DO THIS WORK REQUIRES A LOT OF OPENNESS, WILLINGNESS TO OPEN OLD WOUNDS, & A LOT OF STRENGTH. FOR THE FIRST TIME, I FELT REALLY SEEN & HELD IN MY BROWNNESS & MY FEMMENESS, & ESPECIALLY IN MY FATNESS. AND THIS ALLOWED ME TO WITNESS THESE REALLY INCREDIBLY POWERFUL STORIES THAT ARE SO DESERVING & WORTHY OF BEING HEARD. AND THIS RADICAL ACT OF BEING VULNERABLE ALLOWED ME TO FEEL MORE COMFORTABLE ON STAGE SHARING MY OWN STORIES. IN A WAY, IT FELT LIKE WE WERE CREATING SOMETHING THAT WASN'T ALREADY OUT THERE. SOMETHING THAT I REALLY NEEDED WHEN I WAS A YOUNG, FAT, BROWN GIRL.

I learned my relationship to my body will always be complicated & ambivalent & hard - that just because I performed in this play about fatness doesn't mean that I'm able to love my fat body unconditionally. This work is a never-ending process. I have to give myself gentle reminders that I am enough & worthy & deserving of self-love & self-care.

I think the most significant thing I learned was to not conflate our experiences as fat femmes, that our sizes, gender, race, class, etc., always informs our experiences & the ways in which the world sees us & interacts with us. We're a collective of fat femmes who live at different intersections & our proximity to power & oppression is specific to those intersections.

FROM "FAT: THE PLAY: THE ZINE" WRITTEN BY CALEB LUNA:

"WE REFUSE TO BE AFRAID OF OR DENY THE TRUTHS THAT WE ARE WONDERFUL, BEAUTIFUL, POWERFUL, DESERVING BEINGS. AND SO ARE YOU."

# we are all elders

WRITTEN BY VIVI VERONICA

AS LONG AS I REMEMBER HER, SHE WILL NEVER DIE.

TRANS WOMEN SURVIVE, LOVE, & EXIST BECAUSE OF THE KNOWLEDGE WE PASS DOWN. SHE'S MY SISTER. SHE'S DEAD & ALIVE. SHE'S MY AUNTIE. MY MOTHER. ME.

SHE TAUGHT ME HOW TO MOVE MY FACE, HOW TO CHANGE EVERYTHING WITH MAKEUP, HOW TO MOVE MY BODY IN MOTIONS THAT FELT SO NATURAL. EVEN MY EYES MOVE DIFFERENTLY BECAUSE OF HER. SHE TAUGHT ME THAT

FEAR & COURAGE OFTEN LOOK THE SAME. HOW SITTING WITH UNCERTAINTY IS NECESSARY EVEN IF IT'S PAINFUL.

I FEEL HER IN EVERY PART OF MY BODY—EVEN THE PARTS I HATE—BECAUSE I KNOW HER PAIN & SHE KNOWS MINE.

ALL THE TRANS-FEMININE BODIES & SPIRITS I'VE KNOWN CONTINUE TO TEACH ME. NOT ALL OF MY SISTERS ARE STILL ALIVE, BUT THEIR WISDOM IMPACTS THE FOOTSTEPS OF THOSE STILL HERE. I FEEL OUR ENERGIES MOLDING & SHAPING TO CHANGE WITH EACH OTHER.

THIS WEB OF CONSCIOUSNESS IS SO VAST. I FEEL THE RIPPLES OF THE UNIVERSE FALL DOWN LIKE RAIN UPON ME, & AS THE RAIN TOUCHES ME, MY BODY BECOMES THE RAIN & WASHES ME AWAY INTO THE VASTNESS OF THE WEB. I FEEL YOUR SPIRITS AS THESE RIPPLES & I KNOW YOU ARE FEELING ME TOO. TOGETHER ACROSS THE DIMENSIONS WE UNITE. WE ARE ALL ONE, WE ARE ALL EACH OTHER, & WE ARE ALL THE WISDOM OF OUR SISTERS, OUR ELDERS, OUR SELVES. ONE DAY I DECIDED MY BODY WAS NOT A TRAGEDY.

ON THAT DAY I KNEW I WOULD LIVE FOREVER.

THE NATIONAL COME HOME

A ROUNDTABLE CHAT WITH CEYENNE DOROSHOW & CYD NOVA

MY NAME IS CEYENNE DOROSHOW. I'M A SEX WORKER, SEX WORKER ADVOCATE, A FRIEND, A MOM, A MESS; I'M ALL OF THE ABOVE.

I'M CYD NOVA, I'M JUST A MESSY, UNAFFILIATED HO. IN THE GENERAL SEX WORK WORLD, THERE'S THIS DICHOTOMY OF EITHER BEING "EMPOWERED" BY IT OR "VICTIM" TO IT, & I FEEL LIKE TRANS PPL ARE AT THE CENTER OF THAT NARRATIVE, BECAUSE IF YOU'RE TRANS, YOU'RE GONNA GET FUCKED WITH NO MATTER WHAT.

BECAUSE WE'RE NOT THE "NORM OF SOCIETY" WE'VE HAD TO TURN TO SEX WORK THROUGHOUT HISTORY LONGER THAN ANYONE HAS. WE'RE NOW LIVING IN A WORLD OF ADVOCACY, WHERE IF YOU ARE ONE OF THE PEOPLE PICKED TO WORK AT A NOT-FOR-PROFIT, ANOTHER FORM OF TOKENIZATION, YOU'RE GONNA BE UNDERVALUED & OVERWORKED. SEX WORK ALLOWS US TO HAVE FREEDOM & POWER & BE ABLE TO MAKE THE CALL ON WHAT WE WANT & WILL ACCEPT. WORKING FOR MOST OF THESE NOT-FOR-PROFITS, YOU'RE NORMALLY NOT ALLOWED TO EVEN BE YOURSELF. [IN THE EARLY 1990S] I WORKED FOR THE DEPARTMENT OF HOMELESSNESS WHERE IT WASN'T OKAY FOR ME TO SAY I WAS EVEN TRANS. IF I WERE TO SAY AT THAT MOMENT "I'M TRANSGENDER," WHICH THERE WAS NO WORD FOR IT, THEY WOULD HAVE DEFINITELY FIRED ME.

HOW DID YOU COME INTO DOING SEX WORK?

OH, HOMELESSNESS, SURVIVAL, CENTRAL PARK. I'D GIVEN EVERYBODY ELSE POWER OVER ME. ONE TRICK HAD PAID ME RIDICULOUSLY, & HE SUGGESTED, Y'KNOW THAT, YOU CAN MAKE A LIVING.

BUT ALSO SEX WORK CAN BE THIS GENUINE PATH TO AGENCY THAT CAN BE VERY DIFFICULT TO FIND IN OTHER PLACES.

WHY DO YOU CONTINUE TO DO SEX WORK TODAY?

IT'S EMPOWERING. IT'S GIVEN ME A CHANCE. I DON'T RELY ON CLIENTS LIKE I USED TO BECAUSE OF THE [ADVOCACY] WORK I'M DOING, BUT I CAN DAMN SURE USE WHATEVER I GET TO HELP COMMUNITY.

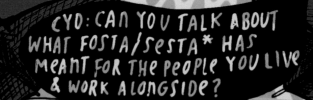

CYD: CAN YOU TALK ABOUT WHAT FOSTA/SESTA* HAS MEANT FOR THE PEOPLE YOU LIVE & WORK ALONGSIDE?

CEYENNE: SINCE SESTA/FOSTA I'VE HAD TO STEP IN AS SORT OF A COUNSELOR TO HELP PEOPLE WITH BREAKING UP, NOT HAVING THE MEANS, WHICH IS CAUSING THE FIGHTS, USING DRUGS. THESE ARE PRIME REJULTS OF SESTA/FOSTA, NOT HAVING THE ABILITY TO ADVERTISE FOR YOUR OWN SURVIVAL, & ITS TAKEN AWAY THEIR LIVELIHOOD & MY LIVELIHOOD IN SO MANY WAYS. I STARTED G.L.I.T.S. [GAYS & LESBIANS LIVING IN A TRANSGENDER SOCIETY] BECAUSE OF THE CHALLENGES FACING COMMUNITY. THE WAYS WE HAD TO PROTECT OURSELVES WE DON'T HAVE ANYMORE & THAT'S ONE OF THE THINGS THAT SESTA/FOSTA CLEARLY TOOK AWAY FROM US. THIS YEAR, THE NUMBER OF TRANSGENDER DEATHS WAS UNPRECEDENTED.

SEX WORK IS REAL WORK!

WHEN YOU PUSH US OFF THE INTERNET YOU FORCE US INTO THE STREETS #STOPSESTA

FOR ME, SEX WORK HAS ALLOWED ME TO DO A LOT OF THAT LIFE WORK STUFF, LIKE EDUCATION & PUTTING MY LIFE IN ORDER IN A WAY THAT I WOULDN'T NECESSARILY HAVE HAD I BEEN WORKING FULL TIME. SO FOR PEOPLE WHO ARE COMING HERE FROM OVERSEAS, HAVE YOU SEEN THE DIFFICULTIES OF SEX WORK IN CURRENT CONDITIONS, WHICH SPECIFICALLY TARGET IMMIGRANTS, IMPACT THEIR ABILITY TO MAKE A LIFE?

# DECRIMINALIZE SEXWORK

I KNOW FOR US, & WE'RE FROM HERE, IT'S NOT EASY. IF I DIDN'T RELY ON MY REGULARS, I WOULDN'T HAVE A ROOF OVER MY HEAD. BUT CERTAINLY FOR THESE PEOPLE COMING FROM OTHER PLACES THEY HAVE THIS DREAM ABOUT SURVIVAL IN A DIFFERENT CITY WHERE THEY'RE FREE, & THEN YOU FIND OUT, NOT SO FREE, IT HURTS.

I SUCCESSFULLY MAINTAINED MY LIFE & HELPED PEOPLE FOR OVER 25 YEARS DOING SEX WORK. SESTA & FOSTA REALLY MADE IT A LOT HARDER. BUT YOU CAN BEST BELIEVE THE LEADERS OF THIS WORLD WILL FIND A WAY TO GET A SEX WORKER. BUT WE, THE SMALL PEOPLE, ARE NOT GONNA BE ABLE TO SURVIVE.

* A BILL SIGNED INTO LAW IN 2018, WHICH WAS BRANDED AS A TOOL TO FIGHT SEX TRAFFICKING BY CRIMINALIZING THE ONLINE SERVICES OR PLATFORM THROUGH WHICH SEX WORKERS ADVERTISE. THE END RESULT WAS MANY POPULAR PLATFORMS ERADICATING ALL SEXUALLY EXPLICIT CONTENT OR DATING PERSONALS & SHUTTING SEVERAL ESCORT WEBSITES DOWN, ENDING PEOPLE'S ACCESS TO WORK OVERNIGHT.

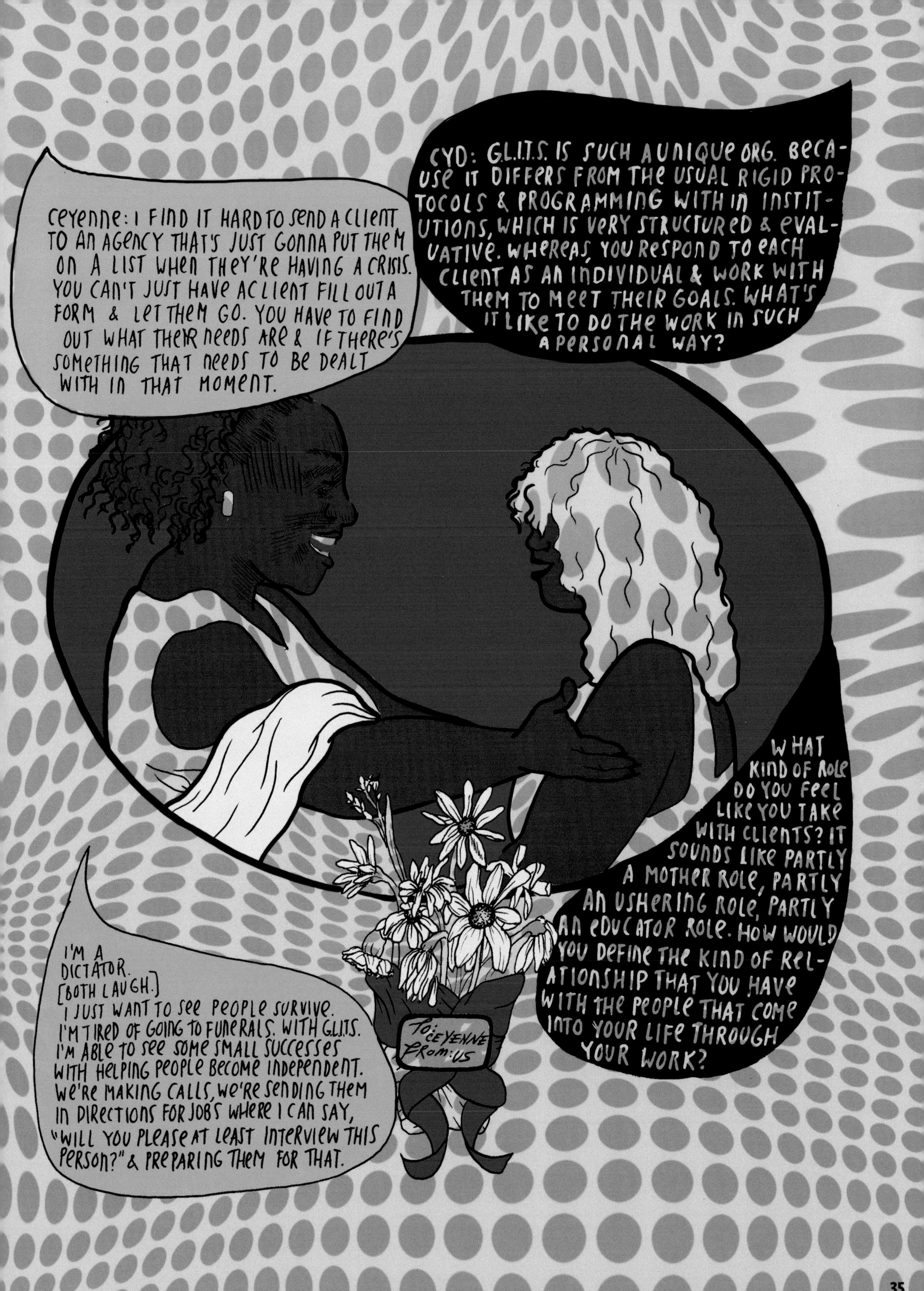

CEYENNE: I FIND IT HARD TO SEND A CLIENT TO AN AGENCY THAT'S JUST GONNA PUT THEM ON A LIST WHEN THEY'RE HAVING A CRISIS. YOU CAN'T JUST HAVE A CLIENT FILL OUT A FORM & LET THEM GO. YOU HAVE TO FIND OUT WHAT THEIR NEEDS ARE & IF THERE'S SOMETHING THAT NEEDS TO BE DEALT WITH IN THAT MOMENT.
CYD: G.L.I.T.S. IS SUCH A UNIQUE ORG. BECAUSE IT DIFFERS FROM THE USUAL RIGID PROTOCOLS & PROGRAMMING WITHIN INSTITUTIONS, WHICH IS VERY STRUCTURED & EVALUATIVE. WHEREAS, YOU RESPOND TO EACH CLIENT AS AN INDIVIDUAL & WORK WITH THEM TO MEET THEIR GOALS. WHAT'S IT LIKE TO DO THE WORK IN SUCH A PERSONAL WAY?
WHAT KIND OF ROLE DO YOU FEEL LIKE YOU TAKE WITH CLIENTS? IT SOUNDS LIKE PARTLY A MOTHER ROLE, PARTLY AN USHERING ROLE, PARTLY AN EDUCATOR ROLE. HOW WOULD YOU DEFINE THE KIND OF RELATIONSHIP THAT YOU HAVE WITH THE PEOPLE THAT COME INTO YOUR LIFE THROUGH YOUR WORK?
I'M A DICTATOR. [BOTH LAUGH.] I JUST WANT TO SEE PEOPLE SURVIVE. I'M TIRED OF GOING TO FUNERALS. WITH G.L.I.T.S. I'M ABLE TO SEE SOME SMALL SUCCESSES WITH HELPING PEOPLE BECOME INDEPENDENT. WE'RE MAKING CALLS, WE'RE SENDING THEM IN DIRECTIONS FOR JOBS WHERE I CAN SAY, "WILL YOU PLEASE AT LEAST INTERVIEW THIS PERSON?" & PREPARING THEM FOR THAT.
TO: CEYENNE FROM: US

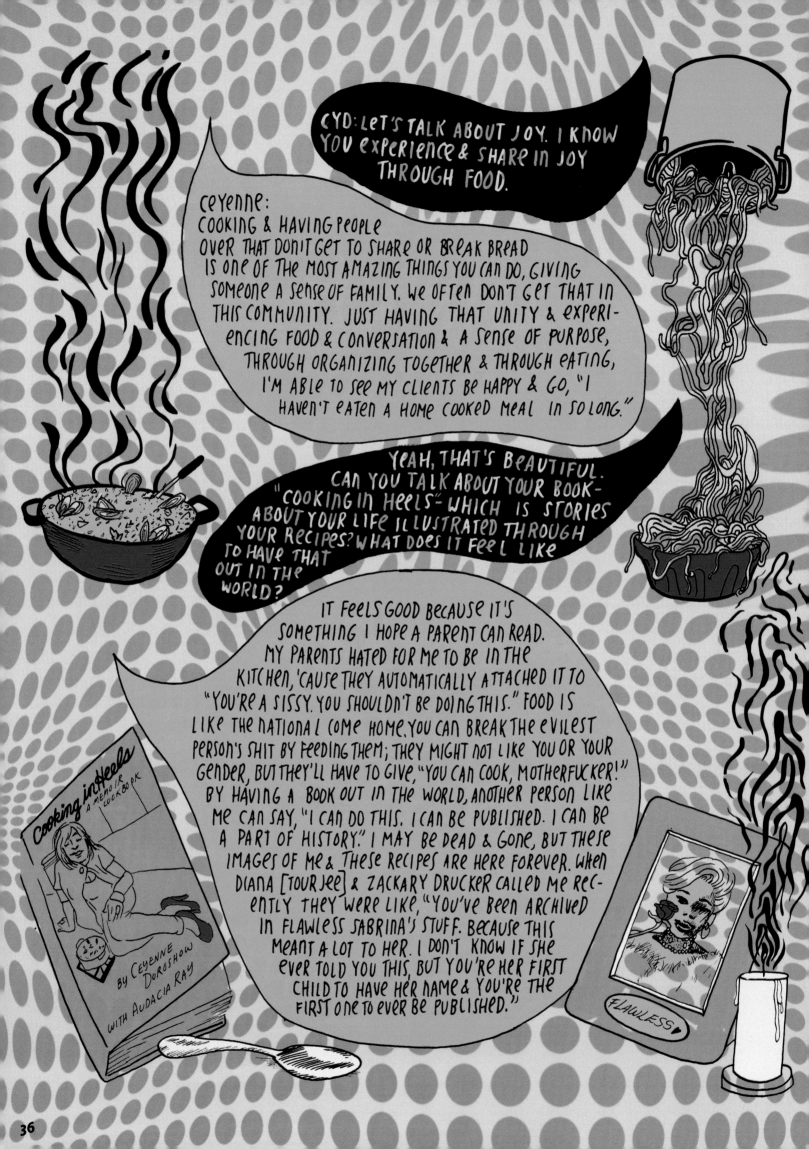

CYD: LET'S TALK ABOUT JOY. I KNOW YOU EXPERIENCE & SHARE IN JOY THROUGH FOOD.

Ceyenne:
COOKING & HAVING PEOPLE OVER THAT DON'T GET TO SHARE OR BREAK BREAD IS ONE OF THE MOST AMAZING THINGS YOU CAN DO, GIVING SOMEONE A SENSE OF FAMILY. WE OFTEN DON'T GET THAT IN THIS COMMUNITY. JUST HAVING THAT UNITY & EXPERIENCING FOOD & CONVERSATION & A SENSE OF PURPOSE, THROUGH ORGANIZING TOGETHER & THROUGH EATING, I'M ABLE TO SEE MY CLIENTS BE HAPPY & GO, "I HAVEN'T EATEN A HOME COOKED MEAL IN SO LONG."

YEAH, THAT'S BEAUTIFUL. CAN YOU TALK ABOUT YOUR BOOK- "COOKING IN HEELS"- WHICH IS STORIES ABOUT YOUR LIFE ILLUSTRATED THROUGH YOUR RECIPES? WHAT DOES IT FEEL LIKE TO HAVE THAT OUT IN THE WORLD?

IT FEELS GOOD BECAUSE IT'S SOMETHING I HOPE A PARENT CAN READ. MY PARENTS HATED FOR ME TO BE IN THE KITCHEN, 'CAUSE THEY AUTOMATICALLY ATTACHED IT TO "YOU'RE A SISSY. YOU SHOULDN'T BE DOING THIS." FOOD IS LIKE THE NATIONAL COME HOME. YOU CAN BREAK THE EVILEST PERSON'S SHIT BY FEEDING THEM; THEY MIGHT NOT LIKE YOU OR YOUR GENDER, BUT THEY'LL HAVE TO GIVE, "YOU CAN COOK, MOTHERFUCKER!" BY HAVING A BOOK OUT IN THE WORLD, ANOTHER PERSON LIKE ME CAN SAY, "I CAN DO THIS. I CAN BE PUBLISHED. I CAN BE A PART OF HISTORY." I MAY BE DEAD & GONE, BUT THESE IMAGES OF ME & THESE RECIPES ARE HERE FOREVER. WHEN DIANA [TOURJEE] & ZACKARY DRUCKER CALLED ME RECENTLY THEY WERE LIKE, "YOU'VE BEEN ARCHIVED IN FLAWLESS SABRINA'S STUFF. BECAUSE THIS MEANT A LOT TO HER. I DON'T KNOW IF SHE EVER TOLD YOU THIS, BUT YOU'RE HER FIRST CHILD TO HAVE HER NAME & YOU'RE THE FIRST ONE TO EVER BE PUBLISHED."

Cooking in Heels
A MEMOIR COOKBOOK
BY CEYENNE DOROSHOW
WITH AUDACIA RAY

FLAWLESS ♥

# QUEER MUSLIM FAMILY
### ✧ A CONVERSATION WITH MIRNA HAIDAR ✧

I AM IN LAW SCHOOL. I'M GRADUATING IN A FEW MONTHS & I FOCUS A LOT ON COMMUNITY BUILDING & PRISON ABOLITION IN MY WORK. I'M A CHAIR COORDINATOR OF THE MUSLIM ALLIANCE FOR SEXUAL & GENDER DIVERSITY, WHICH DOES WORK AROUND QUEER MUSLIM COMMUNITY & THE OTHER ONE IS TARAB NYC, WHICH IS AN ARAB/MENA/SWANA REGION LGBTQ ORGANIZATION THAT I'M CO-CHAIR OF.

I DO A LOT OF WORK AROUND ACCOUNTABILITY PROCESSES, MEANING HOW DO WE BYPASS AN ABUSIVE/OPPRESSIVE INJUSTICE SYSTEM TO REDUCE THE HARM WITHIN OUR COLLECTIVE EXISTENCE? IT PLAYS OUT IN PEOPLE ASKING ME TO MEDIATE OR APPLY SOME ACCOUNTABILITY SKILLS. I GET ASKED TO DO SOME WORKSHOPS SOMETIMES OR FACILITATE DIFFICULT CONVERSATIONS.

RESPECT THE ANCESTORS

In mourning for all those massacred in GAZA

IN LEBANON, I WAS ONE OF THE CO-FOUNDERS OF MEEM, WHICH IS ONE OF THE FIRST LGBTQ ORGANIZATIONS. WE HAD, AT THE TIME I LEFT IN 2010, ABOUT 300 ACTIVE MEMBERS. THEN, I WAS INVITED TO DELIVER A SPEECH AT THE UNITED NATIONS C.O.P. CLIMATE CHANGE BIG CONVENING & STAYED HERE TO APPLY FOR ASYLUM AS [ISRAELI BOMBINGS] ESCALATED IN LEBANON. I HAD $1000 IN MY POCKET & A CARRY-ON. I COUCH SURFED, THEN LIVED IN MY CAR FOR A BIT. AFTER THAT, WHEN I WAS LEGALLY GRANTED PERMISSION TO STAY, I WAS ABLE TO RENT A ROOM IN MICHIGAN & FINISHED MY UNDERGRADUATE AT WAYNE STATE UNIVERSITY WHILE WORKING 2 FULL-TIME POSITIONS.

WHEN I FIRST CAME TO MICHIGAN THERE WAS NO ROOM FOR ME AS A QUEER MUSLIM IN MAINSTREAM LGBTQ ORGANIZATIONS. ALSO IN ARAB ORGANIZATIONS, I FELT COMPLETELY DISREGARDED AS A QUEER MUSLIM. I SAID, "THIS IS UNACCEPTABLE; IT DOESN'T MAKE SENSE THAT WE CAN'T EXIST AS BOTH THESE IDENTITIES." AND THAT'S WHERE I STARTED LOOKING FOR COMMUNITY THAT COULD SHARE THOSE FRAMEWORKS AROUND JUSTICE. I STARTED THE Z COLLECTIVE OUT OF MY BASEMENT IN MICHIGAN, WHICH WAS BASICALLY A PLACE TO HOLD CONVERSATIONS AROUND IDENTITY & FOSTER PROJECTS. IT WAS ALSO A DIRECT RESPONSE TO MEMBERS' OWN PERSONAL EMERGENCIES RELATED TO THEIR IDENTITIES.

UNFORTUNATELY, IN ORGANIZATIONS, LIKE EVEN THE MOST RADICAL ONES, THERE WOULD BE SOME IMMIGRANTS I COULD MEET, BUT IT'S A DIFFERENT KIND OF EXPERIENCE BECAUSE THEY'RE NOT LIKE FIRST GENERATION OR GENERATION ZERO IMMIGRANT. IN MOST LEFTIST ORGANIZATIONS, THERE'S VERY RARELY SOMEONE WHO IS A NEW IMMIGRANT IN A LEADERSHIP POSITION, AND THAT HAS ALWAYS LEFT ME FEELING ALIENATED & ALONE.

ANOTHER CHALLENGE IS HOW DO WE OPERATE AN ECONOMIC JUSTICE MODEL? BECAUSE IT'S REALLY A PRIVILEGE TO BE ABLE TO VOLUNTEER & GIVE TIME TO ENGINEER SUCH A SPACE & THEN WHO ENDS UP SHAPING THE SPACE IS USUALLY PEOPLE WITH PRIVILEGES. FOLKS WHO CAN'T AFFORD TO VOLUNTEER FREE TIME NEED COMPENSATION & ECONOMIC STABILITY.

THE LGBTQ MUSLIM RETREAT IS HOW I CAME TO RECONCILE MY OWN IDENTITIES. FOR 8 YEARS NOW, WE BRING TOGETHER 100+ LGBTQ MUSLIMS FROM ALL OVER THE STATES, CANADA, & LONDON. WE'RE MAJORITY PEOPLE OF COLOR, & WE GATHER IN THE MIDDLE OF THE WOODS IN PENNSYLVANIA. WE HAVE 3 DAYS TOGETHER WHERE WE HEAL TOGETHER. WE ALSO HAVE SOME PROGRAMMINGS LIKE THE TALENT/NO TALENT SHOW, & IT'S SO BEAUTIFUL TO SEE HOW MUCH TALENT THERE IS AMONGST THE COMMUNITY. WE ALSO HAVE A FRIENDS/DATING EVENT WHERE A LOT OF PEOPLE END UP GETTING TOGETHER. IT'S JUST A REALLY MAGICAL, VERY EMOTIONAL PLACE WHERE WHEN WE LEAVE, WE IMMEDIATELY MISS IT & IT FEELS LIKE WE'VE LEFT THE FAMILY BEHIND.

THERE WAS A BABY FOR THE FIRST TIME IN THE RETREAT & WE WERE WORKING ON HAVING SOME CHILDCARE, & I CO-SHARED THAT DUTY WITH SOMEONE NAMED SHAFFIQ. WHEN WE WERE BABYSITTING, WE WERE LIKE, "WHAT DO YOU THINK ABOUT KIDS?" & CHATTING ABOUT IT,

& THEN HE SAID "IT'S MY DREAM TO HAVE A QUEER MUSLIM FAMILY." AND IT REALLY STRUCK ME. THE NEXT DAY, WHEN WE WERE DOING THE FRIENDS/DATING, HE SAID, "WHY DON'T WE TRY TO HAVE A QUEER MUSLIM FAMILY TOGETHER? ME & YOU?" AND NOW FAST FORWARD 5 YEARS, ME & HIM HAVE RUMI & NOAH, THE TWINS, & WE LIVE TOGETHER IN THE SAME HOUSEHOLD, AS A QUEER MUSLIM FAMILY.

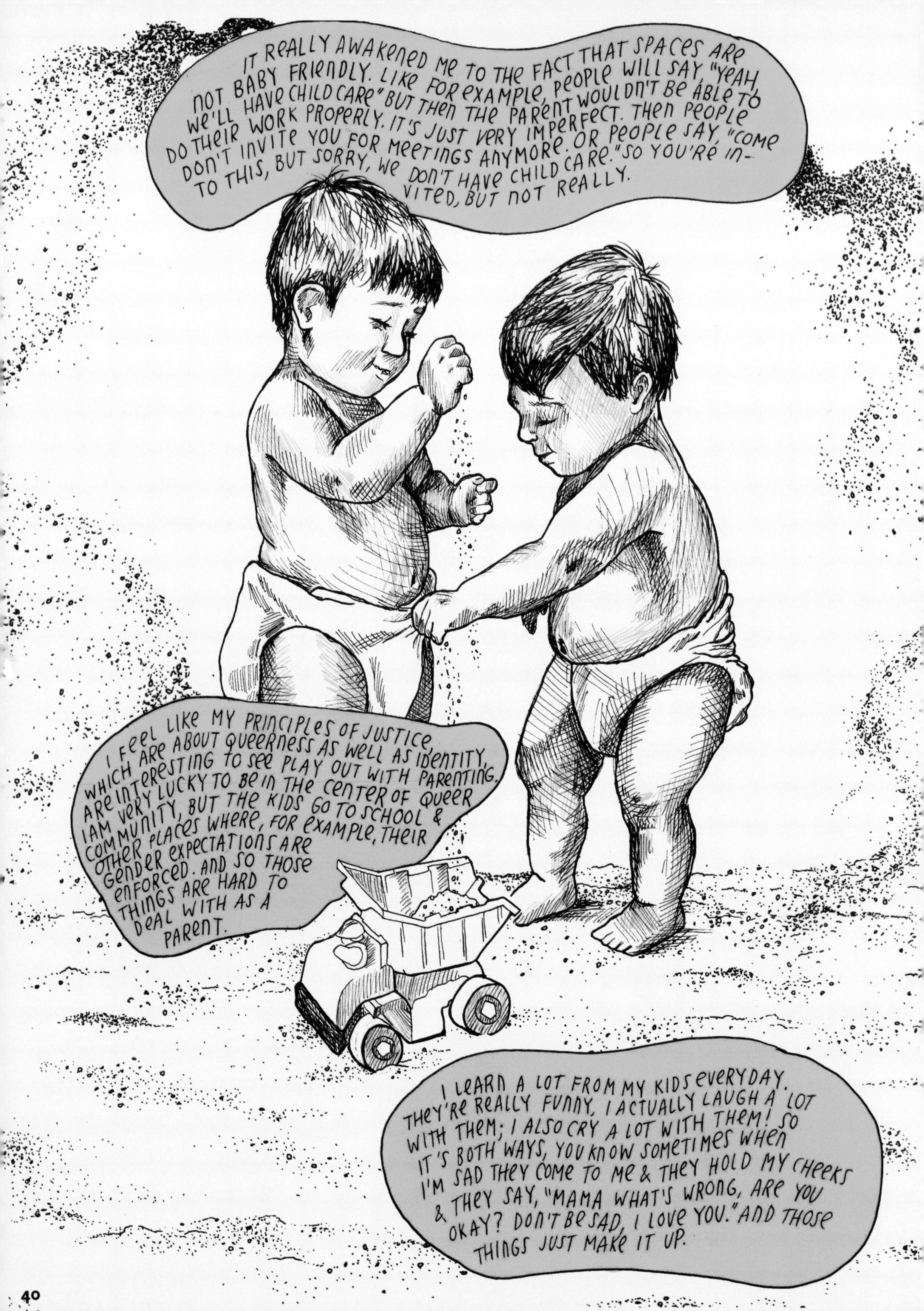
IT REALLY AWAKENED ME TO THE FACT THAT SPACES ARE NOT BABY FRIENDLY. LIKE FOR EXAMPLE, PEOPLE WILL SAY, "YEAH, WE'LL HAVE CHILD CARE" BUT THEN THE PARENT WOULDN'T BE ABLE TO DO THEIR WORK PROPERLY. IT'S JUST VERY IMPERFECT. THEN PEOPLE DON'T INVITE YOU FOR MEETINGS ANYMORE. OR PEOPLE SAY, "COME TO THIS, BUT SORRY, WE DON'T HAVE CHILD CARE." SO YOU'RE INVITED, BUT NOT REALLY.
I FEEL LIKE MY PRINCIPLES OF JUSTICE, WHICH ARE ABOUT QUEERNESS AS WELL AS IDENTITY, ARE INTERESTING TO SEE PLAY OUT WITH PARENTING. I AM VERY LUCKY TO BE IN THE CENTER OF QUEER COMMUNITY, BUT THE KIDS GO TO SCHOOL & OTHER PLACES WHERE, FOR EXAMPLE, THEIR GENDER EXPECTATIONS ARE ENFORCED. AND SO THOSE THINGS ARE HARD TO DEAL WITH AS A PARENT.
I LEARN A LOT FROM MY KIDS EVERYDAY. THEY'RE REALLY FUNNY, I ACTUALLY LAUGH A LOT WITH THEM; I ALSO CRY A LOT WITH THEM! SO IT'S BOTH WAYS, YOU KNOW SOMETIMES WHEN I'M SAD THEY COME TO ME & THEY HOLD MY CHEEKS & THEY SAY, "MAMA WHAT'S WRONG, ARE YOU OKAY? DON'T BE SAD, I LOVE YOU." AND THOSE THINGS JUST MAKE IT UP.

HONESTLY, MY MENTAL STABILITY LIES COMPLETELY ON MY RUNNING SCHEDULE & ON MY CLIMBING. CLIMBING FEELS A BIT MORE COMMUNAL & IT MAKES ME FEEL LIKE I CAN HAVE A STABLE LIFE, DESPITE ALL THE CHALLENGES. I'M CURRENTLY FACING IMMIGRATION CHALLENGES & IT'S JUST REALLY SOMETIMES HARD TO OVERCOME WHILE USHERING THE QUEER MUSLIM COMMUNITY IN A WAY. AND SO, REALLY IF I DIDN'T RUN I WOULD NOT FEEL SANE AT ALL. I JUST RAN THE NYC MARATHON LAST NOVEMBER. I NEVER THOUGHT THAT TO BE POSSIBLE; I ALWAYS TRIED TO RUN FOR ONE MINUTE, 60 SECONDS, & COULDN'T MANAGE & SOMEHOW NOW I RUN FOR HOURS. IT IS A PRIVILEGE & A BLESSING.

MY ARABNESS & MY ROOTS ARE SOMETHING I ALWAYS MISS & I ALWAYS CARRY WITH ME. AND I FEEL LIKE I DON'T BELONG ANYWHERE & THAT'S

ROOTS

THE HARDEST THING TO LIVE WITH AS A REFUGEE. SO THAT'S WHY MY DEFINITION OF HOME NOW IS THROUGH MY

CHOSEN FAMILY, & MY BABIES. BUT THERE'S DEFINITELY ROOTS THAT I'VE MISSED & I FEEL LIKE I'M MISSING ALL THE TIME.

JUST SIMPLY THE ARABIC LANGUAGE, FOR EXAMPLE, LIKE THE ARABIC CALLIGRAPHY SPEAKS VOLUMES TO ME. I HAVE A FEW TATTOOS ON MY BODY, & I HAVE SOME THINGS IN MY ROOM & IN MY OFFICE SET UP AS ARTIFACTS TO CONTINUALLY REMIND ME OF MY ROOTS.

جذور

# EVERYTHING YOU LOVE ABOUT NEW ORLEANS IS BECAUSE OF BLACK PEOPLE

A CONVERSATION WITH PHLEGM

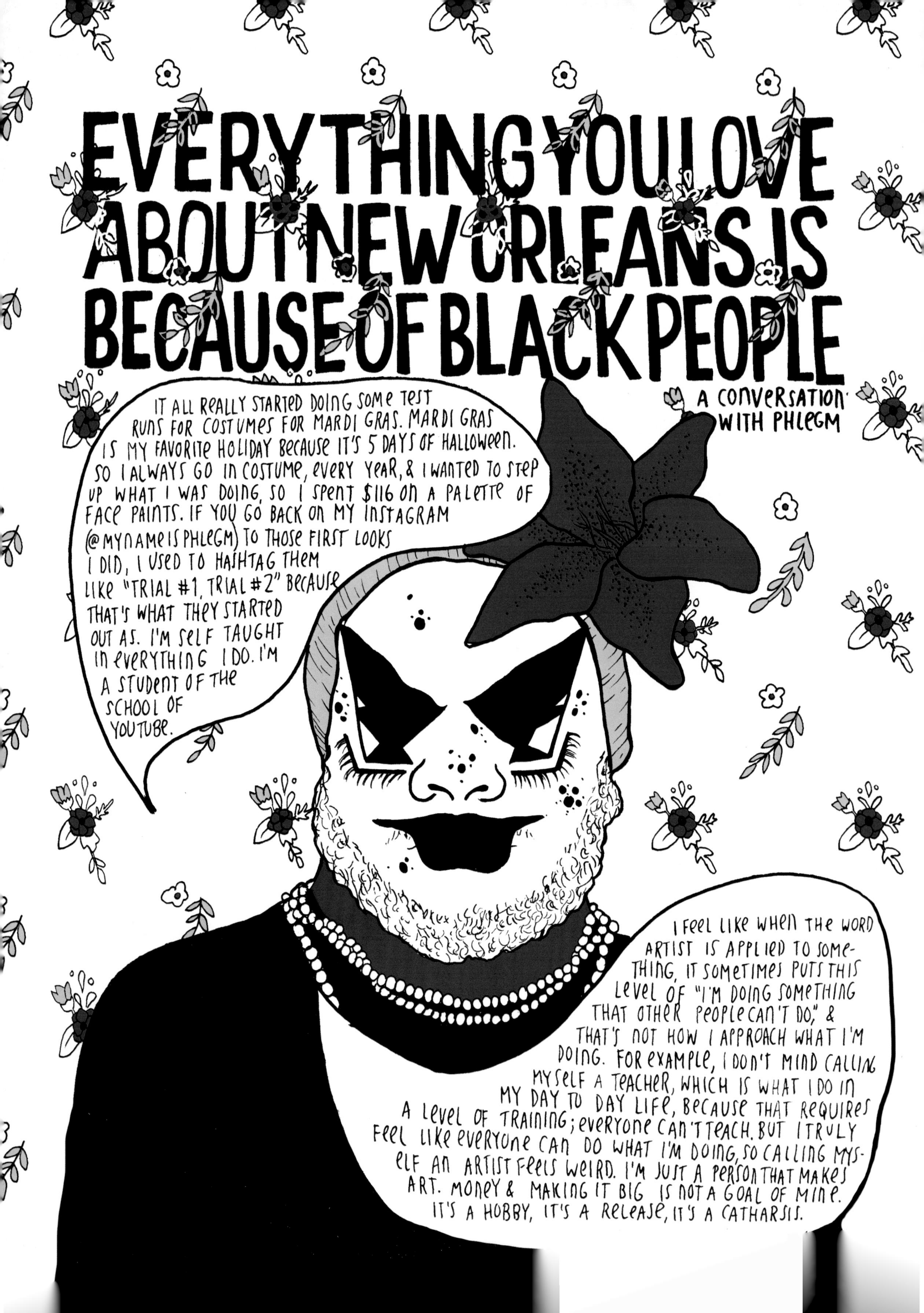

IT ALL REALLY STARTED DOING SOME TEST RUNS FOR COSTUMES FOR MARDI GRAS. MARDI GRAS IS MY FAVORITE HOLIDAY BECAUSE IT'S 5 DAYS OF HALLOWEEN. SO I ALWAYS GO IN COSTUME, EVERY YEAR, & I WANTED TO STEP UP WHAT I WAS DOING, SO I SPENT $116 ON A PALETTE OF FACE PAINTS. IF YOU GO BACK ON MY INSTAGRAM (@MYNAMEISPHLEGM) TO THOSE FIRST LOOKS I DID, I USED TO HASHTAG THEM LIKE "TRIAL #1, TRIAL #2" BECAUSE THAT'S WHAT THEY STARTED OUT AS. I'M SELF TAUGHT IN EVERYTHING I DO. I'M A STUDENT OF THE SCHOOL OF YOUTUBE.
I FEEL LIKE WHEN THE WORD ARTIST IS APPLIED TO SOMETHING, IT SOMETIMES PUTS THIS LEVEL OF "I'M DOING SOMETHING THAT OTHER PEOPLE CAN'T DO," & THAT'S NOT HOW I APPROACH WHAT I'M DOING. FOR EXAMPLE, I DON'T MIND CALLING MYSELF A TEACHER, WHICH IS WHAT I DO IN MY DAY TO DAY LIFE, BECAUSE THAT REQUIRES A LEVEL OF TRAINING; EVERYONE CAN'T TEACH. BUT I TRULY FEEL LIKE EVERYONE CAN DO WHAT I'M DOING, SO CALLING MYSELF AN ARTIST FEELS WEIRD. I'M JUST A PERSON THAT MAKES ART. MONEY & MAKING IT BIG IS NOT A GOAL OF MINE. IT'S A HOBBY, IT'S A RELEASE, IT'S A CATHARSIS.

I THINK AS A KID WHO GREW UP ON THE INTERNET, I REMEMBER BEING 13 OR 14 IN CHAT ROOMS JUST BEING A TROLL. I REMEMBER BEING ON NEOPETS & BEING ON XANGA & LIVEJOURNAL. SO THE INTERNET HAS ALWAYS BEEN A JOKE TO ME, LIKE I NEVER TOOK IT TOO SERIOUSLY. THERE'S THIS SORT OF FLEETINGNESS. INSTAGRAM COULD THEORETICALLY GO OFFLINE TOMORROW & I HAVE NOTHING ON THE INTERNET LEFT OVER. THERE WAS A TIME RECENTLY WHERE I NOTICED MYSELF BEING LIKE, "I HOPE PEOPLE LIKE THIS, I HOPE PEOPLE ENJOY THIS LOOK." IT WAS AROUND THAT TIME THAT I REALLY STARTED TO NOT LIKE THE WORK THAT I WAS PUTTING OUT & I HAD TO RE-CENTER & REMIND MYSELF WHO I'M DOING MY WORK FOR. AT THE END OF THE DAY THE WORK I CREATE IS FOR ME & ME ONLY.

THAT'S HOW I ALWAYS APPROACH SOCIAL MEDIA: AS A PERFORMANCE. THE LOOKS THEMSELVES ARE A PIECE OF ART. AND THEN THE CAPTIONS ARE ALSO. EVEN IF IT'S FOR 15 SECONDS WHEN YOU STOP, LIKE THE PICTURE, THEN SCROLL PAST, I JUST WANT YOU TO BE ABLE TO BE IN THAT MOMENT, & NOT BE THINKING ABOUT WHATEVER THE FUCK ELSE IS GOING ON, LIKE IF YOU HAVE FUCKING PUT YOUR BANK ACCOUNT IN THE RED FOR LIKE ANOTHER MONTH, OR SHIT IS SUCKING & IT'S MISERABLE.

FOR THOSE 15 SECONDS I JUST WANT PEOPLE TO BE ABLE TO FORGET ABOUT WHATEVER.

As a New Orleans native, I really really like bald cypress trees with the hanging moss. When I see them either further out in the swamps or in the city itself, I always stop & stare at them because they are sort of spooky & haggard & raggedy but also pretty & timeless.

Something very Southern Gothic about a bald cyprus. Those kinds of things influence my work.

Through the use of self-portraiture & mixed media face painting, I really want to pay direct homage to native African religious & cultural practices. My work is deeply rooted in the ritual & sanctity of African religious face paint & masking. It is a contemporary veneration of ancestors. An ocular calling of the corners. A visual invocation of the spirit. An optic reclamation of space.

# The Wild Hunt Ride

## A CONVERSATION WITH AMBER KIM

Rainy day. Cousins at our house for a visit. So we decide to do rainy day games. Eventually someone has the idea to have all the boys dress as girls & the girls dress as boys.

It was my first chance to be a fairie princess & damned if I wasn't gonna take it.

I would spend hours upon hours in the woods, because when you're alone, it doesn't matter what you are.

IT WAS AROUND THIS TIME THAT I STARTED TO READ THE ENCYCLOPEDIA BECAUSE, EVEN THOUGH I STILL DIDN'T KNOW ANYTHING THAT WASN'T PROTESTANT APPROVED, I WAS FINALLY SEEING THE SEAMS WHERE THINGS HAD BEEN ARTFULLY REMOVED FROM THE WORLD.

IT TOOK ME UNTIL MIDDLE SCHOOL TO GET TO THE LETTER "T."

I TRIED TO MOVE OUT OF MY PARENTS' HOUSE ON MULTIPLE OCCASIONS. GOT THWARTED BY MY PARENTS EVERY TIME. GETTING BEATEN DIDN'T BREAK ME. BEING EMOTIONALLY TOYED WITH DIDN'T BREAK ME. HAVING TO HIDE MY GENDER, POLITICS, RELIGIOUS BELIEFS, MY SOUL, DIDN'T BREAK ME. HAVING THE HOPE THAT I COULD LEAVE & LIVE MY LIFE PROVEN TO BE FALSE BROKE ME. I HAD A FULL PSYCHOTIC EPISODE.

I HAVE NOW SPENT A DECADE IN PRISON.

THERE IS ONE THING THAT I DISCOVERED THAT REALLY FREAKED ME OUT CONSIDERING THAT I HAVE A SPIRITUAL CONNECTION TO THE FAE. DECEMBER 5TH IS THE FIRST NIGHT OF THE YEAR THAT, ACCORDING TO FOLKLORE, THE WILD HUNT RIDES. THIS IS ALSO THE SAME NIGHT THAT I BROKE. COULD BE COINCIDENCE, OR IT COULD BE THAT DUE TO MY WEAKNESS FATE DECIDED TO TAKE A HAND.

MY NUMBER ONE SURVIVAL STRATEGY HAS ALWAYS BEEN OBSERVE & UNDERSTAND. I DON'T DEFINE THINGS LIKE TRUST IN THE SAME WAY MOST PEOPLE DO. MOST PEOPLE WOULD SAY TRUST MEANS KNOWING SOMEONE WILL ALWAYS ACT IN YOUR BEST INTEREST.

TO ME, TRUST MEANS KNOWING HOW A PERSON WILL ACT GIVEN A PARTICULAR STIMULUS. THUS, FOR ME TO TRUST SOMEONE I MUST BE ABLE TO OBSERVE THEIR BEHAVIOR OVER A PERIOD OF TIME

AND UNDERSTAND WHY THEY DO WHAT THEY DO. THE SAME APPLIES TO INSTITUTIONS, SOCIAL CONSTRUCTS, & BELIEF SYSTEMS. THIS WAS SEMI-USEFUL IN SCHOOL & HAS BECOME AN ABSOLUTELY MANDATORY SURVIVAL STRATEGY IN PRISON.

I HOPE TO SOME DAY GET OUT SO I CAN LIVE MY LIFE AS THE STRONG, EMPOWERED, WITCHY WOMAN I AM MEANT TO BE. AND I PRAY THAT THIS TIME THE PRICE OF HOPE WAS WORTH IT.

# ~ita

con cariño, liberando la comunidad QTBIPOC una plantita a la vez.

with love, liberating the QTBIPOC community one plant at a time.

## AUTHORED BY
## STEPH NIAUPARI (THEY/ELLE)
### SPANISH TRANSLATION: PLANTITA POWER LANGUAGE TEAM
### ASL VERSION: EMMA V. BALDERAS (SHE/ELLA)

¿Cuándo fue la última vez que bebiste agua?
¿Cuándo fue la última vez que observaste su propio cuerpx y admiraste como creces?
¿Te has fijado en el espacio que has creado para ti mismx?
¿Has eliminado las cosas que ya no te dan provecho?
¿Sabes lo que necesitas para prosperar?

Las plantas se hacen estas preguntas todos los días. Encuentran nuevas formas de prosperar con o sin atención constante. Son un tributo, un momento de alegría, un recordatorio de lo que somos capaces de sobrevivir a pesar de las condiciones.

When was the last time you drank water?
When was the last time you looked at your own body and admired its growth?
Have you checked in with the space you've created for yourself?
Have you removed the items that no longer work for you?
Do you know what you need in order to thrive?

Plants ask themselves these questions every day. They find new ways to thrive with or without constant care. They are a tribute, a moment of joy, a reminder of what we are able to survive despite the conditions.

COMO PLANTAS, TAMBIén SOMOS NUESTRXS PROPIOS SANADORES, IMAGÍNENSE SI RECORDAMOS SER TAN AMABLES CON NOSOTRXS MISMXS. CUANDO NOS HACEMOS ESTAS PREGUNTAS, ESTAMOS RECONOCIENDO QUE LOS SISTEMAS QUE NOS RODEAN NO PUEDEN CONTENERNOS.

AS PLANTS, WE ARE ALSO OUR OWN HEALERS —IMAGINE IF WE REMEMBERED TO BE JUST AS KIND TO OURSELVES. WHEN WE ASK OURSELVES THESE QUESTIONS, WE ARE RECOGNIZING THE SYSTEMS THAT SURROUND US CANNOT CONTAIN US.

VIVIMOS EN UN MUNDO QUE DESAFÍA Y ATACA CONTINUADAMENTE NUESTRX PODER TODOS LOS DÍAS, Y AÚN DEBEMOS RECORDAR QUE LA LUCHA NO DEBE SER UN REQUISITO PREVIO PARA LA ALEGRÍA.

WE LIVE IN A WORLD THAT CHALLENGES AND ACTIVELY ATTACKS OUR POWER EVERY SINGLE DAY, AND STILL WE MUST REMEMBER THAT STRUGGLE SHOULD NOT BE A PREREQUISITE TO JOY.

49

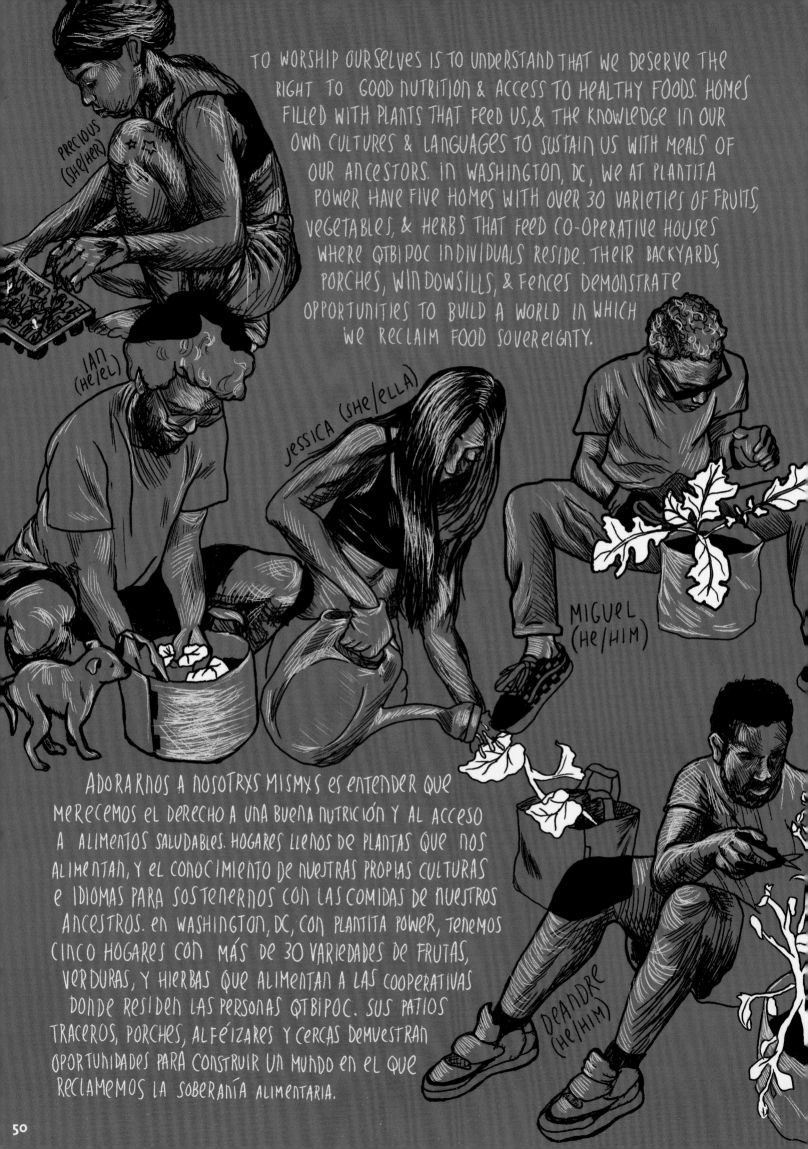

TO WORSHIP OURSELVES IS TO UNDERSTAND THAT WE DESERVE THE RIGHT TO GOOD NUTRITION & ACCESS TO HEALTHY FOODS. HOMES FILLED WITH PLANTS THAT FEED US, & THE KNOWLEDGE IN OUR OWN CULTURES & LANGUAGES TO SUSTAIN US WITH MEALS OF OUR ANCESTORS. IN WASHINGTON, DC, WE AT PLANTITA POWER HAVE FIVE HOMES WITH OVER 30 VARIETIES OF FRUITS, VEGETABLES, & HERBS THAT FEED CO-OPERATIVE HOUSES WHERE QTBIPOC INDIVIDUALS RESIDE. THEIR BACKYARDS, PORCHES, WINDOWSILLS, & FENCES DEMONSTRATE OPPORTUNITIES TO BUILD A WORLD IN WHICH WE RECLAIM FOOD SOVEREIGNTY.

PRECIOUS (SHE/HER)

IAN (HE/EL)

JESSICA (SHE/ELLA)

MIGUEL (HE/HIM)

DEANDRE (HE/HIM)

ADORARNOS A NOSOTRXS MISMXS ES ENTENDER QUE MERECEMOS EL DERECHO A UNA BUENA NUTRICIÓN Y AL ACCESO A ALIMENTOS SALUDABLES. HOGARES LLENOS DE PLANTAS QUE NOS ALIMENTAN, Y EL CONOCIMIENTO DE NUESTRAS PROPIAS CULTURAS E IDIOMAS PARA SOSTENERNOS CON LAS COMIDAS DE NUESTROS ANCESTROS. EN WASHINGTON, DC, CON PLANTITA POWER, TENEMOS CINCO HOGARES CON MÁS DE 30 VARIEDADES DE FRUTAS, VERDURAS, Y HIERBAS QUE ALIMENTAN A LAS COOPERATIVAS DONDE RESIDEN LAS PERSONAS QTBIPOC. SUS PATIOS TRASEROS, PORCHES, ALFÉIZARES Y CERCAS DEMUESTRAN OPORTUNIDADES PARA CONSTRUIR UN MUNDO EN EL QUE RECLAMEMOS LA SOBERANÍA ALIMENTARIA.

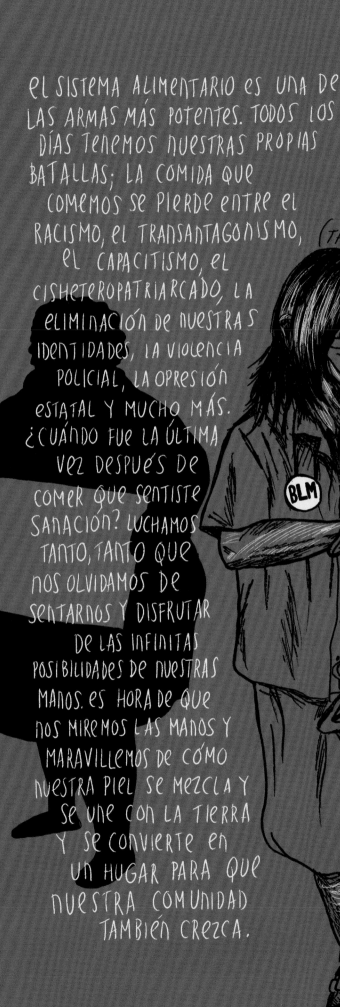

EL SISTEMA ALIMENTARIO ES UNA DE LAS ARMAS MÁS POTENTES. TODOS LOS DÍAS TENEMOS NUESTRAS PROPIAS BATALLAS; LA COMIDA QUE COMEMOS SE PIERDE ENTRE EL RACISMO, EL TRANSANTAGONISMO, EL CAPACITISMO, EL CISHETEROPATRIARCADO, LA ELIMINACIÓN DE NUESTRAS IDENTIDADES, LA VIOLENCIA POLICIAL, LA OPRESIÓN ESTATAL Y MUCHO MÁS. ¿CUÁNDO FUE LA ÚLTIMA VEZ DESPUÉS DE COMER QUE SENTISTE SANACIÓN? LUCHAMOS TANTO, TANTO QUE NOS OLVIDAMOS DE SENTARNOS Y DISFRUTAR DE LAS INFINITAS POSIBILIDADES DE NUESTRAS MANOS. ES HORA DE QUE NOS MIREMOS LAS MANOS Y MARAVILLEMOS DE CÓMO NUESTRA PIEL SE MEZCLA Y SE UNE CON LA TIERRA Y SE CONVIERTE EN UN HUGAR PARA QUE NUESTRA COMUNIDAD TAMBIÉN CREZCA.

ANDY (THEY/ELLE)

THE FOOD SYSTEM IS ONE OF THE MOST POTENT WEAPONS. EVERY DAY WE HAVE OUR OWN BATTLES; THE FOOD WE EAT BECOMES LOST BETWEEN RACISM, TRANSANTAGONISM, ABLEISM, CISHETEROPATRIARCHY, ERASURE OF OUR IDENTITIES, POLICE VIOLENCE, STATE OPPRESSION, & SO MUCH MORE. WHEN WAS THE LAST TIME YOU FELT HEALED AFTER EATING A MEAL? WE FIGHT FOR SO LONG, FOR SO MUCH, WE FORGET TO SIT DOWN & ENJOY THE ENDLESS POSSIBILITIES OF OUR HANDS & MARVEL AT HOW OUR SKIN BLENDS WITH THE SOIL & BECOMES A HOME FOR OUR COMMUNITY TO GROW TOO.

BLM

# DEFUND MPD with PUPUSAS WE FEED US! @PLANTITAPOWER

WASHINGTON, DC, SE HA CONVERTIDO EN UN PARAÍSO GASTRONÓMICO SOLO PARA LOS COLONIZADORES, LOS GENTRIFICADORES, LOS CIS BLANCOS QUE OCUPAN ESPACIOS ENCERRADOS EN VENTANAS TAN ALTAS QUE PUEDEN IGNORAR LA VIOLENCIA QUE PROVOCAN A DIARIO. DEJAN AL RESTO EN UN ESCASEZ DE COMIDA, UN CONCEPTO QUE SE EXTIENDE MÁS ALLÁ DE UN ÁREA GEOGRÁFICA, SON COMUNIDADES QUE SOLO COMEN LECHUGA EN LAS HAMBURGUESAS DE MACDONALD, SOLO TIENEN ACCESO A ARÁNDANOS EN LOS MUFFINS DE 7-ELEVEN, Y NO TIENEN LA OPCIÓN DE PAGAR POR INSTACART. PARA LA COMUNIDAD QTBIPOC, LA DISCRIMINACIÓN ES UN DESIERTO EN QUE LES ASIGNAN UN GÉNERO DE FORMA INCORRECTA EN LOS SUPERMERCADOS, REVIVE LA DISFORIA AL IR A LAS DESPENSAS DE ALIMENTOS Y SE LES RECHAZA LAS PROTECIONES LEGALES CREANDO BARRERAS SOCIALES Y ECONÓMICAS.

WASHINGTON, DC, HAS BECOME A FOOD PARADISE ONLY FOR THE SETTLERS, THE GENTRIFIERS, THE WHITE CIS PEOPLE WHO OCCUPY SPACES ENCLOSED IN WINDOWS SO HIGH THAT THEY CAN IGNORE THE VIOLENCE THEY CAUSE DAILY. IT LEAVES THE REST OF US IN A FOOD DESERT; A CONCEPT THAT STRETCHES BEYOND A GEOGRAPHICAL AREA, IT IS COMMUNITIES THAT ONLY EAT LETTUCE FROM MCDONALD'S BURGERS, CAN ONLY AFFORD BLUEBERRIES IN 7-ELEVEN MUFFINS, & DO NOT HAVE THE OPTION OF PAYING FOR INSTACART. FOR THE QTBIPOC COMM- UNITY, DISCRIMINATION IS THE DESERT THAT MISGENDERS THEM AT SUPERMARKETS, RELIVES DYSPHORIA WHEN GOING TO FOOD PANTRIES, & REFUSES LEGAL PROTECTIONS FROM SOCIAL & ECONOMIC BARRIERS.

STEPH NIAUPARI (THEY / ELLE)

WATER 4 THE REVOLUTION
FOOD 4 RESISTANCE
+FREE BINDERS
BECAUSE WE'RE FUCKING FABULOUS

VEGGIES
CUCUMBERS
PARSLEY
SWISS CHARD

SQUASH
NT ME
EEKS
ME LOTS
+ ♡

SUMMER SQUASH
TRANSPLANT ME IN
1-2 WEEKS
GIVE ME LOTS
OF ☼ + LOVE

THE
FATE
OF
NUTRITIONAL
ACCESS FALLS
ONCE MORE AS RESPONSIBILITY
TO OUR OWN COMMUNITIES.
WITHOUT FOOD, WE CANNOT CONTINUE TO
FIGHT FOR OUR COLLECTIVE JOY. SO WHEN WE
TOGETHER BUILD THESE GARDENS IN THE HOMES
OF QTBIPOC INDIVIDUALS WE REPEAT,

¿CUÁNDO FUE LA ÚLTIMA VEZ QUE BEBISTE AGUA?
¿CUÁNDO FUE LA ÚLTIMA VEZ QUE OBSERVASTE SU
PROPIO CUERPX Y ADMIRASTE COMO CRECES? ¿TE
HAS FIJADO EN EL ESPACIO QUE HAS CREADO
PARA TI MISMX? ¿HAS ELIMINADO
LAS COSAS QUE YA NO TE DAN
PROVECHO? ¿SABES LO QUE
NECESITAS PARA PROSPERAR?

LET THE PLANTS AND YOUR
HANDS FIND THE
HEALING YOU NEED
STEPH
(THEY/ELLE)

EL
FUTURO
DEL ACCESSO
NUTRICIONAL
VUELVE A SER NUESTRA
RESPONSIBILIDAD ENTRE LAS
COMUNIDADES. SIN COMIDA,
NO PODEMOS SEGUIR LUCHANDO
COLECTIVAMENTE POR NUESTRA ALEGRÍA. ENTONCES,
CUANDO JUNTXS CONSTRUIMOS ESTOS JARDINES EN LAS
CASAS DE LAS PERSONAS DE QTBIPOC, REPETIMOS,

WHEN WAS THE LAST TIME YOU DRANK WATER?
WHEN WAS THE LAST TIME YOU LOOKED AT YOUR OWN
BODY AND ADMIRED ITS GROWTH? HAVE YOU
CHECKED IN WITH THE SPACE YOU'VE CREATED
FOR YOURSELF? HAVE YOU REMOVED THE
ITEMS THAT NO LONGER WORK FOR
YOU? DO YOU KNOW WHAT YOU NEED
IN ORDER TO THRIVE?

DEJA QUE LAS PLANTAS Y
TUS MANOS ENCUENTREN
LA SANACIÓN
QUE NECESITAS PARA
TO SET YOU
LIBERARTE.
FREE.

NAJMA
(THEY/ELLE)

FOR
ASL
TRANSLATION,

SCAN
THIS
QR CODE.

# AURIGA [1]
## BY JAYE SABLAN

BEFORE FIRST CONTACT
YOU & I

EMERGED FROM OUR
BODIES
TO
FOLLOW
AMARANTHINE
BELLS RINGING

AT THE
HORNED MOUTH
OF A TERRESTRIAL
ISLAND

# BECOMING REAL
## A CONVERSATION WITH JAYE SABLAN

I'M REALLY THINKING THROUGH STARTING HORMONES MORE SERIOUSLY. BUT I'M NOT NECESSARILY GOING TO CHANGE THE WAY I DRESS. MY GENDER IS TOMBOY. I'M MISREAD AS A CIS GAY MALE ALL THE TIME, & SOME PEOPLE FEEL LIKE THEY CAN RELATE TO ME BECAUSE THEY HAVE CERTAIN ASSUMPTIONS ABOUT MY IDENTITIES.

I'M QUEER, NOT JUST IN MY SEXUALITY, BUT ALSO POLITICALLY. WHEN I SAY I HAVE QUEER POLITICS IT MEANS WHAT DOES SOCIAL JUSTICE, SOLIDARITY, & LIBERATION MEAN FOR INDIGENOUS FOLKS, BLACK FOLKS, TRANS WOMEN OF COLOR, CIS WOMEN OF COLOR, FOLKS WITH DISABILITIES, WORKING CLASS & IMMIGRANT FOLKS, & YES, QUEER COMMUNITIES TOO—ALL THE INTERSECTIONS?

AND THERE
WITH GILDED
NETS;

WOVEN WITH
THE SILVERY
HAIRS OF OUR
FOREMOTHERS

WE CAUGHT

MOLTEN SLAG

SWELLING

SKYWARD

MY POETRY IS A SPACE WHERE I CAN BE MY WHOLE SELF. IT'S A SPACE WHERE I CAN NUTURE & PROTECT ALL OF WHO I AM. I AM GENDERQUEER AND AN INDIGENOUS CHAMORU FEMINIST & NO-BODY CAN QUESTION THAT.

WRITING HAS SAVED MY LIFE MORE THAN ONCE SINCE I WAS YOUNG. I'VE BEEN HOSPITALIZED IN PSYCHIAT-RIC WARDS SEVERAL TIMES BECAUSE OF DEPRESSION & ATTEMPTS AT SUICIDE. FOR ME, POETRY IS SELF-CARE, ONE OF THE MOST IMPORTANT TOOLS I HAVE TO SURVIVE.

AND NOT JUST TO SURVIVE,
BUT TO THRIVE.

TO CAST US LIGHT-
STREAMING ACROSS
A FIELD OF STARS
& INTO
THE CLUSTERED PALM
OF
AURIGA[1]

MY POEM "AURIGA" IS MY TAKE ON SCI-FI FUTURISM THAT IS ALSO ROOTED IN THE PAST. IN IT, I TRY TO REFERENCE MY INDIGENOUS CHAMORU PEOPLE'S ANCIENT COSMOLOGY & SPIRITUALITY, THINGS THAT I HAVE LEARNED & RESEARCHED ON MY OWN. BEING & LIVING IN THE DIASPORA MEANS THAT I AM GRASPING AT PIECES OF A PUZZLE TO MAKE SENSE OF MY CULTURE, HISTORY, & FUTURE. I THINK THIS POEM IS AN EXAMPLE OF THAT. I'VE ALWAYS FOUND THE FLAME TREE REALLY BEAUTIFUL, ESPECIALLY ITS BLOSSOMS. IT CAN BE FOUND ON THE MARIANA ISLANDS WHERE I'M FROM. & THERE'S A REALLY OLD CHAMORU STORY BEHIND HOW THE TREE CAME TO BE—A TRAGIC LOVE STORY. A YOUNG MAN & WOMAN WERE FORBIDDEN TO SEE EACH OTHER BECAUSE THEIR FAMILIES DIDN'T GET ALONG. OF COURSE THEY CONTINUED TO SEE EACH OTHER, BUT IT BECAME INCREASINGLY DIFFICULT. THEY DECIDED TO TAKE THEIR OWN LIVES, STABBING
EACH OTHER
BY A TREE.

AURIGA,
A MASSIVE
STAR CONSTE-
LLATION, WAS
RECORDED IN PICT-
OGRAPH FORM BY MY
ANCESTORS THOUSANDS OF
YEARS AGO IN THE RITIDIAN
CAVES OF GUAHAN. PAINTED IN
DEEP RED, AURIGA IS DEPICTED
AS AN OPEN-FACED HAND WITH
FINGERS SPREAD APART. NOT ONLY
DO STARS HAVE IMMENSE SPIRITUAL
POWER IN ANCIENT CHAMORU COSMO-
OGY, THEY HELPED MY ANCESTORS NAVI-
GATE SEAFARING JOURNEYS.

THEIR BLOOD
POURED &
SEEPED INTO THE
GROUND, THEN
THE ROOTS OF THE
TREE, EVENTUALLY
REACHING THE BLOSSOMS.
THE PETALS WENT FROM
WHITE TO FIERY
RED.

# We Give Money To Trans People

A ROUNDTABLE INTERVIEW WITH THE FOUNDING MEMBERS OF TRANS ASSISTANCE PROJECT (TAP)

When TRUMP GOT elected, I WAS SITTING WITH MY FRIEND MARY, & WE WERE JUST LIKE "TRANS PEOPLE ARE GOING TO LOSE ALL OF THEIR RIGHTS IN THE NEXT 4 YEARS. WE DON'T EVEN HAVE RIGHTS NOW, BUT IT'S GONNA GET WORSE. WE'RE GONNA HAVE LEGISLATION PASSED AGAINST US ACTIVELY." THERE WAS THIS WOMAN ON TWITTER—I DON'T KNOW WHO SHE IS—WHO MADE A POST THAT SAID "I WILL PAY FOR ANY TRANS PERSON'S PASSPORT UNTIL I RUN OUT OF MONEY. JUST MESSAGE ME." I MESSAGED HER, & SHE IMMEDIATELY GOT BACK TO ME, & JUST ASKED, "HOW MUCH?" NO OTHER QUESTIONS. THAT MADE ME THINK, OH, THERE'S ACTUALLY A LOT OF PEOPLE WHO WOULD BE WILLING TO FINANCIALLY SUPPORT TRANS PEOPLE IF THERE WAS AN EASIER WAY TO DO IT. THAT WAS A LIGHT BULB MOMENT; THAT IT'S POSSIBLE TO REDISTRIBUTE FUNDS IN A WAY THAT TRUSTS TRANS PEOPLE.

WE STARTED NOV. 10TH, & BY THANKSGIVING DAY, WE MADE OUR CROWDFUNDING SITE ACTIVE. AT THAT POINT WE HAD OVER 500 PEOPLE SIGN UP. WE GOT IN WITH THE Q CENTER & PARTICIPATED IN AN I.D. CLINIC THEY PUT TOGETHER, & WE GAVE OUT SOMETHING LIKE $5000. PEOPLE'S FACES WERE LIGHTING UP, BECAUSE THEY WERE LIKE, "NO ONE'S EVER JUST GIVEN ME MONEY. EVERYONE WANTS ME TO PROVE I'M TRANS OR ASKS ME FOR RECEIPTS FOR THINGS I CAN'T AFFORD." PEOPLE ARE ALWAYS WANTING THINGS FROM TRANS PEOPLE, LIKE LETTERS FROM PSYCHIATRISTS, WITHOUT UNDERSTANDING HOW DIFFICULT THEY ARE TO GET.

Bunny

twitter

JULES

IT'S NO SECRET THAT QUEER & TRANS FOLKS HAVE ALWAYS HAD MANY BARRIERS UP AROUND FINANCES. WE ARE REDISTRIBUTING RESOURCES WITHOUT GATEKEEPING. MEANING THAT WE ACTUALLY DON'T ASK PEOPLE WHO WE'RE WORKING WITH THAT MANY QUESTIONS. WE ASK THEM BASIC CONTACT INFO, TELL THEM WHAT WE'RE DOING, BUT MOSTLY THE CALL IS GIVING THEM TIME TO TALK ABOUT WHAT THEY WANT TO SEE HAPPEN. WE'RE REDISTRIBUTING RESOURCES IN A WAY THAT'S BASED IN SELF-DETERMINATION.

BUT ALSO, IT'S IMPORTANT FOR US TO BE REAL ABOUT HAVING THAT POSITION, WHICH IS A POSITION OF POWER, TO HAVE ACCESS TO THAT MONEY & TO BE REDISTRIBUTING IT. WE'RE REALLY TRYING TO BUILD THIS PROJECT OUT OF OUR POLITICS, ETHICS, & INTEGRITY. ESPECIALLY AS AN ORGANIZATION MOSTLY RUN BY WHITE PEOPLE, IT TAKES TIME, FEEDBACK, & CHALLENGING ONE ANOTHER TO EFFECTIVELY CREATE PROGRAMS THAT, FOR EXAMPLE, GIVE STIPENDS TO TRANS PEOPLE WHO ARE OR HAVE BEEN INCARCERATED OR ARE SEX WORKERS.

We have a lot of people donate art or put on shows for us. We've gotten a few grants; we've raised money from some big social media pushes. And I want us to be really conscious about the way we build our social media page, like, who are we boosting? When we decided to do a fundraising campaign for trans commissary funds, for example, we were really thinking about what kinds of communities we would be impacting. We also want to be intentional about how we use our social media to elevate voices & facilitate dialogue among the trans community.

STELLA

It's been really important for us to build our values & our intention for longevity into the very structure of the org early on. For me, recharging is really important. I try to remember why I'm doing this; it connects to why I'm visibly trans & queer. It's not just for my own happiness, it's also because there are people who, just by seeing me, might be more kind to queer people in the future. Or if they are queer, they might feel less alone or come out sooner.

I'M A FORMER SEX WORKER, HIV+, & HAVE IDENTIFIED AS NON-BINARY & FEMME FOR ABOUT 5 YEARS NOW. I GREW UP IN VIRGINIA, WHERE SYSTEMS OF OPPRESSION LOOK MORE BLUNT & UNDILUTED THAN THE PASSIVENESS OF THE WEST COAST. THAT SHAPED MY WAY COMING INTO THIS WORK, BECAUSE I'VE HAD TO NAVIGATE THOSE SYSTEMS. A BIG THING WE'RE WORKING ON IS BREAKING DOWN THE POWER DYNAMIC OF HAVING RESOURCES PEOPLE WANT. THE MORE TRANSPARENT WE ARE, THE MORE PEOPLE ARE LIKE, "THANK YOU FOR YOUR HONESTY INSTEAD OF BEATING AROUND THE BUSH." WE HAVE TO QUESTION & DECONSTRUCT THESE SYSTEMS & BRAINSTORM WAYS TO MAKE THEM MORE ACCESSIBLE. THINKING OUTSIDE THE BOX & TRYING TO PLACE YOURSELF IN DIFFERENT PERSPECTIVES IS KEY IN DOING THIS WORK IN A WAY THAT BENEFITS EVERYONE.

PHOS

**BUNNY:**

I WANT TO BE CLEAR THAT WE'RE NOT SAVIORS OF THE TRANS COMMUNITY. WE'VE MADE MISTAKES & WE'RE ALWAYS LEARNING. ONE OF THE THINGS I'VE BEEN STEERING US TOWARD AS THE DIRECTOR IS ACTUALLY HAVING LESS POWER. I DON'T WANT TO BE THE PERSON MAKING DECISIONS ABOUT HOW MUCH MONEY TO ALLOT TO TRANS PEOPLE WHO HAVE SPENT TIME IN PRISON OR FACE RACIAL DISCRIMINATION OR HAVE TO NAVIGATE IMMIGRATION, BECAUSE I'M NOT A PART OF THOSE COMMUNITIES. THAT'S ALSO WHY WE GIVE MONEY TO OTHER ORGS WHO SHOULD BE MAKING THOSE DECISIONS, NOT US. OUR PRIVILEGE NOW IS THAT WE HAVE A FUNDRAISING MACHINE THAT IS ABLE TO GENERATE WEALTH, SO I WANT TO USE THAT PRIVILEGE TO GET TO A PLACE WHERE WE DON'T HAVE TO BE DOING THIS anymore.

# MARTIAL ARTS IS THE MOST FLUENT ASIAN LANGUAGE I SPEAK

A CONVERSATION WITH ANABEL KHOO & SZE-YANG ADE-LAM

SZE-YANG: I'VE BEEN DOING MARTIAL ARTS FOR A REALLY LONG TIME. I STARTED WHEN I WAS 12 OR 13, & BEFORE THAT IT WAS ALWAYS PRESENT IN MY LIFE. I WAS BULLIED. I GREW UP IN VANCOUVER & WE WERE LIVING IN A MIDDLE-CLASS AREA BUT WE WERE NOT MIDDLE CLASS. WHEN I WENT TO ELEMENTARY SCHOOL, A LOT OF WHITE KIDS TRIED TO PICK ON ME BECAUSE I WAS SMALLER & ASIAN, BUT THEY WERE MIDDLE-CLASS KIDS THAT DIDN'T REALLY KNOW HOW TO FIGHT, & I CAME FROM A VIOLENT HOUSEHOLD, SO ENDED UP BEATING BACK THE BULLIES. TO COPE WITH A LOT OF THE DOMESTIC VIOLENCE IN MY HOME, I IMAGINED EVERY DAY WAS A BIG ADVENTURE. I THOUGHT, "MY HORRIBLE PARENTS ARE LIKE THESE GIANT MONSTERS & I HAVE TO SURVIVE THEM, & RUN AROUND, FIGHT BAD GUYS, & PROTECT THE ONES I LOVE." IT WAS MY WAY TO MAKE SENSE OF THINGS IN A FAIRY TALE SETTING. AND FROM THERE, I STARTED TAE KWON DO.

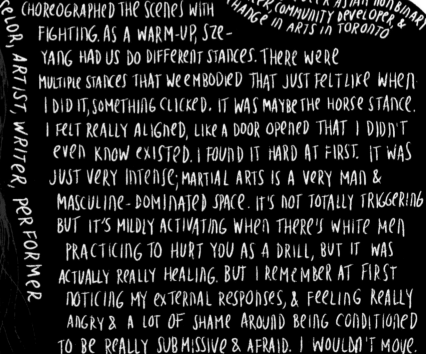

SZE-YANG ADE-LAM: I AM QUEER ASIAN NONBINARY MARTIAL ARTIST, DANCER, COMMUNITY DEVELOPER, & ADVOCATE FOR CHANGE IN ARTS IN TORONTO

ANABEL: I STARTED KUNG FU BECAUSE OF SZE-YANG. I WAS AN ACTOR IN A PLAY THAT OUR FRIEND WROTE & SZE-YANG CHOREOGRAPHED THE SCENES WITH FIGHTING. AS A WARM-UP, SZE-YANG HAD US DO DIFFERENT STANCES. THERE WERE MULTIPLE STANCES THAT WE EMBODIED THAT JUST FELT LIKE WHEN I DID IT, SOMETHING CLICKED. IT WAS MAYBE THE HORSE STANCE. I FELT REALLY ALIGNED, LIKE A DOOR OPENED THAT I DIDN'T EVEN KNOW EXISTED. I FOUND IT HARD AT FIRST. IT WAS JUST VERY INTENSE; MARTIAL ARTS IS A VERY MAN & MASCULINE-DOMINATED SPACE. IT'S NOT TOTALLY TRIGGERING BUT IT'S MILDLY ACTIVATING WHEN THERE'S WHITE MEN PRACTICING TO HURT YOU AS A DRILL, BUT IT WAS ACTUALLY REALLY HEALING. BUT I REMEMBER AT FIRST NOTICING MY EXTERNAL RESPONSES, & FEELING REALLY ANGRY & A LOT OF SHAME AROUND BEING CONDITIONED TO BE REALLY SUBMISSIVE & AFRAID. I WOULDN'T MOVE. I WOULD HAVE THIS COMPLETE FREEZE RESPONSE.

ANABEL KHOO, HOLISTIC MENTAL HEALTH COUNSELOR, ARTIST, WRITER, PERFORMER

SY: I feel really fortunate to have grown up with kung fu & kung fu cinema— especially the strong womyn of kung fu film. I think having these two things saved me & kept me safer. In almost every space I enter, the expectation is that I'm weaker, incompetent, & unintelligent. Almost every insult when ur perceived as male is being called a woman or queer & thus weak. Kung fu is a space where the perceived Asian male body is seen as POWERFUL & A SOURCE OF UNLIMITED POTENTIAL. IT'S NOT PERFECT BY ANY MEANS; IT CAN BE SEX-IST, HOMOPHOBIC; OFTEN IT'S NOT INCLUSIVE OR ACCESSIBLE; IT'S VERY ABILITY-BASED. BUT IN THIS PARTICULAR SPACE, & HAVING IMAGES OF POWERFUL WOMYN LIKE MICHELLE YEOH, I HAD A PART OF LIFE WHERE I WAS SEEN AS AND I KNEW I WAS POWERFUL & STRONG.

AK: I FELT REALLY ALONE & REALLY WEIRD IN TERMS OF CHILDHOOD STUFF. I WAS BORN IN MALAYSIA. I'M CHINESE, BUT WE IMMIGRATED TO CANADA WHEN I WAS THREE, & I'VE BEEN SUPER DISCONNECTED FROM CHINESE CULTURE. I DIDN'T KNOW ABOUT ANYTHING LIKE KUNG FU, & IT WAS NEVER A THING I THOUGHT OF DOING. I JUST FELT LIKE IT BELONGED TO ME BUT IT DIDN'T, & IT DIDN'T FEEL LIKE I DESERVED TO BE THERE. BUT IT ALSO FELT SO IMPORTANT. FELT THIS FAMILIARITY, LIKE MY BODY WAS LIKE, "FINALLY, SHE FOUND HER WAY BACK HOME." [WING CHUN] IS THE FORM OF KUNG FU WE'RE CURRENTLY TRAINING IN. I REALLY LIKE THE LEGEND OF IT. THERE WAS THIS GIRL WHO WAS BEING PURSUED BY THIS CREEPY WARLORD WHO WAS LIKE, "YOU HAVE TO MARRY ME" & SHE DIDN'T WANT TO, & SHE GETS HELP FROM THIS WARRIOR MONK LADY WHO TRAINS HER, & THEN SHE GOES & KICKS THIS GUY'S ASS.

SY: I GOT INTO WING CHUN BECAUSE I WANTED TO DO SOMETHING THAT WAS REALLY PRACTICAL. AS A QUEER NONBINARY ASIAN PERSON, WHO IS OFTEN PERCEIVED AS A BOY OR MALE, & WHOSE SEXUAL & ROMANTIC LIFE HAS OFTEN BEEN LINKED TO MEN, I HAVE EXPERIENCED THE RACISM & SEXUAL HARASSMENT THAT EXISTS IN THE GAY WORLD. FROM MEN (NOT EXCLUSIVELY BUT MOST OFTEN WHITE) TRYING TO DRAG ME OR MY FRIENDS AWAY AT CLUBS & TOUCHING ME UNCONSENSUALLY, TO HOOKUPS THAT GO FROM GOOD TO BAD REAL FAST, KUNG FU GAVE ME THE SENSE OF BOLDNESS TO SAY NO, & WHEN NO WASN'T ENOUGH, I'VE HAD TO PUNCH A FEW MEN & SAY THINGS LIKE, "IF YOU DON'T STOP, I'LL BREAK YOUR FACE." MEN SEEM SO SHOCKED AT THE NOTION THAT AN ASIAN PERSON HAS THE ABILITY TO REFUSE, & IF THEY CONTINUE TO PHYSICALLY PURSUE, ARE EVEN MORE SHOCKED THAT AN ASIAN WOULD FIGHT FOR THEMSELVES. THESE MOMENTS HAVE ALWAYS LEFT ME WITH THE SCARY & SAD THOUGHTS OF THE FOLKS THAT DIDN'T OR COULDN'T SAY NO OR DEFEND THEMSELVES. THAT'S ONE OF THE REASONS I CONTINUE TO DEEPEN MY KNOWLEDGE & SHARE PRACTICAL MARTIAL ARTS WITH QTBIPOC FOLKS, CAUSE I KNOW THE REALITIES OF DANGER, & THAT IT AFFECTS OTHERS EVEN MORE THAN ME.

SY: I THINK FOR ASIAN FOLKS THERE'S SO MUCH SHAME THAT WE HOLD, ESPECIALLY WITH STUFF LINKED TO OUR CULTURE, LIKE LOSING OUR NATIVE TONGUE. LIKE WE SHOULD ALREADY KNOW. WHITE FOLKS ARE LIKE, "I CAN SPEAK JAPANESE, KOREAN, CHINESE." THEY DON'T FEEL THE BAGGAGE OF LEARNING A NEW LANGUAGE; IT'S JUST FUN FOR THEM. SADLY THIS OFTEN LEAVES US DISCONNECTED FROM OUR ROOTS, BUT NOT ON MY WATCH. GROWING UP I WAS CONSTANTLY TOLD, "YOU'RE NOT CHINESE, YOU'RE TOO DARK," BOTH BY MY EXTENDED FAMILY & BY THE COMMUNITIES IN VANCOUVER.

MARTIAL ARTS IS THE MOST FLUENT ASIAN LANGUAGE I SPEAK.

PERFORMING KUNG FU IS THE ONLY TIME I AM CLAIMED BY THE CHINESE COMMUNITY IN A POSITIVE WAY. WHEN I'M PRACTICING WING CHUN OR OTHER FORMS OF MARTIAL ARTS, I FEEL A DEEP ANCESTRAL CONNECTION. KUNG FU & MARTIAL ARTS IN ASIA IS SUCH A LARGE PART OF STORYTELLING & EXPRESSION. ASIANS FLIRT WITH KUNG FU, MEDITATE WITH KUNG FU, PLAYFULLY INTERACT, VIOLENTLY INTERACT, IT'S SUCH A HUGE PLATFORM TO EXPRESS SO MANY DIFFERENT STORIES.

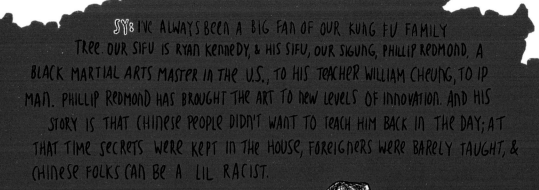

SY: I'VE ALWAYS BEEN A BIG FAN OF OUR KUNG FU FAMILY TREE. OUR SIFU IS RYAN KENNEDY, & HIS SIFU, OUR SIGUNG, PHILLIP REDMOND, A BLACK MARTIAL ARTS MASTER IN THE U.S., TO HIS TEACHER WILLIAM CHEUNG, TO IP MAN. PHILLIP REDMOND HAS BROUGHT THE ART TO NEW LEVELS OF INNOVATION. AND HIS STORY IS THAT CHINESE PEOPLE DIDN'T WANT TO TEACH HIM BACK IN THE DAY; AT THAT TIME SECRETS WERE KEPT IN THE HOUSE, FOREIGNERS WERE BARELY TAUGHT, & CHINESE FOLKS CAN BE A LIL RACIST.

SO SIGUNG REDMOND LEARNED CANTONESE IN A CHINESE RESTAURANT IN NYC, WAS FINALLY ACCEPTED, & CHANGED THE COURSE OF HISTORY. I APPRE-CIATE THAT OUR TREE IS REALLY DIVERSE IN REGARDS TO DIFFERENT PEOPLE: PEOPLE OF COLOR, BLACK PEOPLE, INDIGENOUS PEOPLE, & THAT OUR TEACHER, WHO'S AMAZING, HAS TAUGHT US IN WAYS THAT SEE US AS FULL BEINGS, WITHOUT ANY HIERARCHICAL BULLSHIT.

I HOPE TO QUEERIFY THE FUTURE GENERATIONS, STARTING WITH A SMALL QUEER TRANS NONBINARY ASIAN CONTIGENT, THAT I PLAYFULLY CALL A QUEER ASIAN KUNG FU GANG, OR SWORD SISTERS.

USUALLY, THE FORMS HAVE A CONCEPT. SO THE FIRST FORM IS CALLED SIU NIM TAU; I THINK IT TRANSLATES TO "LITTLE THOUGHTS IN THE HEAD." IT'S SINGLE ARM MOVEMENTS, WHERE YOU'RE LEARNING HOW TO ISOLATE & KNOW WHERE YOUR ENERGY IS. THE NEXT FORM IS CALLED CHUM KIU; THE CONCEPT OF THAT ONE IS "SEEKING THE BRIDGE" OR "SINKING THE BRIDGE." IT'S WHEN 2 POINTS CONTACT, SO WHEN YOU CONTACT THE OTHER PERSON'S HAND, & "I'M GOING TO MOVE THIS ARM BECAUSE I KNOW WHERE I FEEL THE CONTACT POINT."

I THINK THAT'S THE BEAUTIFUL CONCEPT, LIKE YOU'RE CONNECTED TO THIS PERSON FOR A MOMENT SO YOU'RE GONNA TRY TO FIGURE OUT HOW TO GET ON TOP OF IT, HOW TO MANEUVER IT. THEN THE FORM AFTER THAT—THERE'S THESE INTERESTING SUCCESSIONS OF GROWTH AS YOU GET DEEPER INTO IT— IS CALLED BIU JEE. BIU JEE IS LIKE SOME-THING WENT WRONG; IT HAS A LOT MORE ELBOWS TO THE FACE & EYE GOUGES. I THINK IT TRANSLATES TO "DARTING FINGERS" BUT I TRANSLATE IT TO "WHEN SHIT HITS THE FAN."

**SY:**
FOR A LOT OF QTBIPOCS, WE LIVE IN
FIGHT-OR-FLIGHT. WE'RE SO USED TO FIGHT-
ING, EVEN WITH EACH OTHER SOMETIMES,
WHICH IS UNFORTUNATE, BUT IT HAPPENS
TOO 'CAUSE WE'RE AT SUCH A HIGH
FREQUENCY. SO ONE OF THE THINGS THAT
WING CHUN GIVES IS PRACTICING HOW TO STAY
CALM & NOT ESCALATE. THERE ARE A LOT OF
PLACES IN BETWEEN 0 & 100 THAT WE CAN
DIAL IN TO, SO THAT WE DON'T HAVE TO
GO RIGHT TO 100, & WHATEVER THAT TRIGGERS
IN US. HOW DO WE SINK, HOW DO WE RETURN TO
A PRACTICE THAT'S PHYSICAL, THAT'S GROUNDED.

**AK:** I'VE BEEN DRAWING A LOT OF LESSONS
& INSPIRATION FROM KUNG FU IN HOW
I'M TRYING TO THINK OF & PRACTICE
RESISTANCE, REVOLUTION, & HEALING.
ONE LESSON IS ON RECEIVING SUPPORT, &
THE OTHER IS ON FLOWING TOWARD
TRANSFORMATION.

BRUCE LEE WROTE ABOUT
YIELDING, QUOTING THE TAO TE
CHING: "THE STRONG &
MIGHTY TOPPLE FROM THEIR
PLACE & THE SOFT &
YIELDING RISE ABOVE THEM ALL."
WHEN WE HEAR THE WORD
"YIELDING," IT CAN BE
UNDERSTOOD AS A HOLDING
BACK OR GIVING UP, BUT THE
WAY BRUCE LEE DESCRIBED IT,
& THE WAY I'VE EXPERIENCED
IT IN WING CHUN, "YIELDING" IS A
TUNING INTO HOW THE EARTH
LONGS TO SUPPORT YOU. IN
PSYCHOTHERAPEUTIC CON-
TEXT, THERE'S A
PRACTICE CALLED
"YIELDING" THAT REFERS TO A
MINDFUL SENSING & RECEIVING
SUPPORT FROM LOVED ONES, THE LAND
& OUR BODIES. I FEEL LIKE THERE
IS AN ENERGY OF DELIBERATION &
A TUNING IN THAT IS REALLY
NECESSARY TO SUSTAINABLE &
TRANSFORMATIVE CHANGE.

AK:
ONE OF MY FAVORITE WING CHUN MOVES IS CALLED PO PAI JEUNG, WHICH REFERS TO CARRYING THE SIGN WITH THE NAME OF THE DECEASED IN A FUNERAL. IT'S A DOUBLE PALM MANEUVER THAT MOVES LIKE WATER, "SOFTLY" AT FIRST, SENSING ITS WAY AROUND OBSTACLES, THEN ENDS WITH A POWERFUL STRIKE. IT DEMONSTRATES THE SHAPE-SHIFTING QUALITY OF WATER & THE MINDFULNESS THAT MOVEMENTS FOR SOCIAL CHANGE HOLD & NEED, & IT REMINDS ME OF HOW BRUCE LEE DESCRIBED WATER:

"NOTHING IN THE WORLD IS MORE YIELDING & SOFTER THAN WATER; YET IT PENETRATES THE HARDEST. INSUBSTANTIAL, IT ENTERS WHERE NO ROOM IS. IT IS SO FINE THAT IT IS IMPOSSIBLE TO GRASP A HANDFUL OF IT; STRIKE IT, YET IT DOES NOT SUFFER HURT; STAB IT, & IT IS NOT WOUNDED... IF YOU TRY TO REMEMBER YOU WILL LOSE. EMPTY YOUR MIND, BE FORMLESS, SHAPELESS. LIKE WATER. NOW YOU PUT WATER IN A CUP, IT BECOMES A CUP. YOU POUR WATER INTO A BOTTLE, IT BECOMES THE BOTTLE... NOW WATER CAN FLOW OR CREEP OR DRIP—OR CRASH! BE WATER, MY FRIEND."
—THE TAO OF GUNG FU" BY BRUCE LEE.

WITH KUNG FU, YOU'RE MOVING THE LIFE FORCE OF THE COSMOS WITH & AROUND YOUR BODY, WHICH OFFERS A REGENERATIVE WAY OF APPROACHING CHANGE THAT'S VERY DIFFERENT THAN A CAPITALIST PARADIGM THAT FORCES US TO WORK OURSELVES TO THE GROUND & COMPETE IN A CULTURE OF SCARCITY THAT MAY "REWARD" US IF WE "DESERVE IT ENOUGH." WHEN I MOVE THROUGH PO PAI JEUNG, I FEEL LIKE WE ALREADY HAVE EVERYTHING WE NEED FOR ANOTHER BETTER WORLD; ONE THAT WE DESERVE & DESPERATELY NEED. NOT ONLY CAN I FEEL THAT IT'S POSSIBLE, I CAN SENSE THAT IT'S ALREADY HERE, WAITING FOR US TO JUST LET IT FLOW.

# PEOPLE'S MEDICINE

A conversation with Geleni Fontaine

MY GRANDMOTHER WAS KIND OF A MEDICINE WOMAN IN CUBA & DID A LOT OF HEALING, & LEARNED FROM HER MOTHER & HER GRANDMOTHER, & THESE WERE THINGS I NEVER GOT TO LEARN FROM HER. SO IT'S REALLY PLEASING TO BE ABLE TO PRACTICE A SIMILAR KIND OF MEDICINE & KIND OF CARRY IT FORWARD IN MY OWN LIFE. SHE USED TO PICK HERBS IN PROSPECT PARK IN BROOKLYN WHEN I WAS A KID.

ORIGINALLY THE THING THAT REALLY INTERESTED ME WAS HERBAL MEDICINE, & ACUPUNCTURE WAS SOMETHING I TRIED BECAUSE I WAS DEALING WITH MY OWN ILLNESS. I WAS DEALING WITH REALLY SEVERE ANEMIA & WAS HAVING REALLY HEAVY PERIODS & GETTING DEPLETED & VERY FATIGUED WHEN I WAS IN MY 20s. AND I HAD ACUPUNCTURE WHICH IMMEDIATELY LIFTED MY ENERGY IN A WAY THAT I WAS ALMOST SUSPICIOUS OF. I WAS DOING ANTI-VIOLENCE WORK & PROGRAMMING WITH YOUTH. AND WHEN I WAS IN BETWEEN JOBS AT ONE POINT I GOT REALLY SICK & JUST CRASHED & COULDN'T DO ANYMORE. I THOUGHT, "THIS IS THE TIME; LET ME GO BACK TO SCHOOL."

THIRD ROOT STARTED IN 2008 AS A HOLISTIC HEALING SPACE WITH THE PRIMARY THING ABOUT IT BEING THAT IT WAS COLLECTIVELY RUN. OUR SPACE IS IN THE STOREFRONT OF A LITTLE PLACE IN DITMAS PARK WHICH IS ALSO KNOWN AS A FLATBUSH NEIGHBORHOOD IN BROOKLYN & IT'S A REALLY MULTICULTURAL NEIGHBORHOOD & THE NEXUS OF A LOT OF DIFFERENT COMMUNITIES. WE WORK REALLY HARD TO BE A SPACE THAT'S ACCESSIBLE & EMPOWERING & COLLABORATIVE FOR COMMUNITY. THERE ISN'T THE SENSE THAT WE, WHO ARE DOING THE HEALING WORK, ARE THE ABSOLUTE EXPERTS. ACCESS, SLIDING SCALE FEES, SCHOLARSHIP PROGRAMS ARE CENTRAL TO WHAT WE DO.

thirdroot

IF YOU LOOK INTO THE HISTORY OF THE DIFFERENT HEALING MOVEMENTS, YOU FIND THAT SOCIAL JUSTICE ASPECT & VICE VERSA. ALONDRA NELSON WROTE AN AMAZING BOOK ABOUT THE BLACK PANTHERS & THE HISTORY AROUND CREATING HEALTH JUSTICE MOVEMENTS THAT WERE ACCESSIBLE. AND ACUPUNCTURE HAD A DEEP HISTORY THAT CAME THROUGH THE BLACK PANTHERS & SOCIAL JUSTICE MOVEMENTS BEFORE THE U.S. OR NIXON EVER WENT TO CHINA. ACUPUNCTURE WAS PEOPLE'S MEDICINE & IT WAS PUT INTO A CONTEXT IN WHICH THERE WERE HEALTHCARE CENTERS, PEOPLE COMING IN FOR FREE, PEOPLE GETTING TRAINED TO DO IT REALLY QUICKLY & EFFECTIVELY & BEING ABLE TO SHARE IT WITH EACH OTHER. THIS WAS ALWAYS COMMUNITY-BASED MEDICINE & IT WAS ALWAYS PART OF AN UNDERSTANDING OF WHAT LIBERATION COULD BE FOR PEOPLE. THIS HAS ALWAYS BEEN PEOPLE'S MEDICINE TO ME.

[DURING] THE LAST NOLOSE CONFERENCE, WHICH ORIGINALLY WAS A NONPROFIT GROUP THAT WAS ABOUT FAT QUEER COMMUNITIES ORGANIZING & CREATING VIBRANT CULTURE TOGETHER, I WAS ONE OF A GROUP OF PEOPLE THAT PUT TOGETHER A HEALING JUSTICE PRACTICE SPACE. THE FIRST COUPLE OF DAYS OF THE CONFERENCE WAS REALLY FOCUSED ON & ONLY INCLUDED BLACK, INDIGENOUS, & PEOPLE OF COLOR COMMUNITIES.

SUPERFAT

NOLOSE HAS BEEN A REALLY LOVELY COMMUNITY THAT'S GIVEN SPACE FOR PEOPLE TO REALLY EXPLORE THE IDEA OF WHAT IT MEANS TO BE IN A TRANSGRESSIVE BODY AT A TIME WHEN FAT PEOPLE, IN PARTICULAR, ARE SEEN AS DISEASED.

I FEEL LIKE ONE OF THE VERY BASIC THINGS THAT BEING A HEALER WITH CHRONIC PAIN DOES FOR ME IS THAT IT HELPS ME BE AWARE OF MY OWN ENERGY IN A WAY THAT'S REALLY HELPFUL. BEING CONSCIOUS OF EVERY STEP, BECAUSE IF I'M NOT, I COULD FALL DOWN OR INJURE MYSELF. I REALLY CONSIDER THE PHYSICAL SPACE I'M IN & WHAT'S GOING TO BE THE MOST COMFORTABLE FOR PEOPLE INCLUDING MYSELF. I DON'T SUPRISE SOMEONE WHO'S MAYBE NERVOUS ABOUT TREATMENT FOR THE FIRST TIME. I USE MY OWN LANGUAGE TO GAUGE MY ENERGY & BRING MY FOCUS IN. "DO I NEED TO STRAIGHTEN OUT MY LEG?" "IS THAT GIVING ME PAIN RIGHT NOW?" "OH, OKAY. I'M GONNA MOVE OVER THIS WAY."
AS I WAS FIRST STARTING TO DEAL WITH MORE DISABILITY, I THOUGHT IT WAS GOING TO GET IN THE WAY A LOT, & THERE ARE THINGS THAT ARE DIFFICULT. THERE ARE A LOT OF LOGISTICS TO MANAGE, BUT IN TERMS OF ACTUAL PRACTICING ONE ON ONE WITH PEOPLE IT ACTUALLY BRINGS ME CLOSER. THERE IS SOMETHING ABOUT MOVING THROUGH PAIN & ILLNESS & DEALING WITH YOUR OWN STUFF THAT HONES YOU TO BE ABLE TO SUPPORT OTHER PEOPLE DOING THE SAME.

TAMEICKA "IFASINA" CLEAR

GALADRIEL MOZEE LEGARE

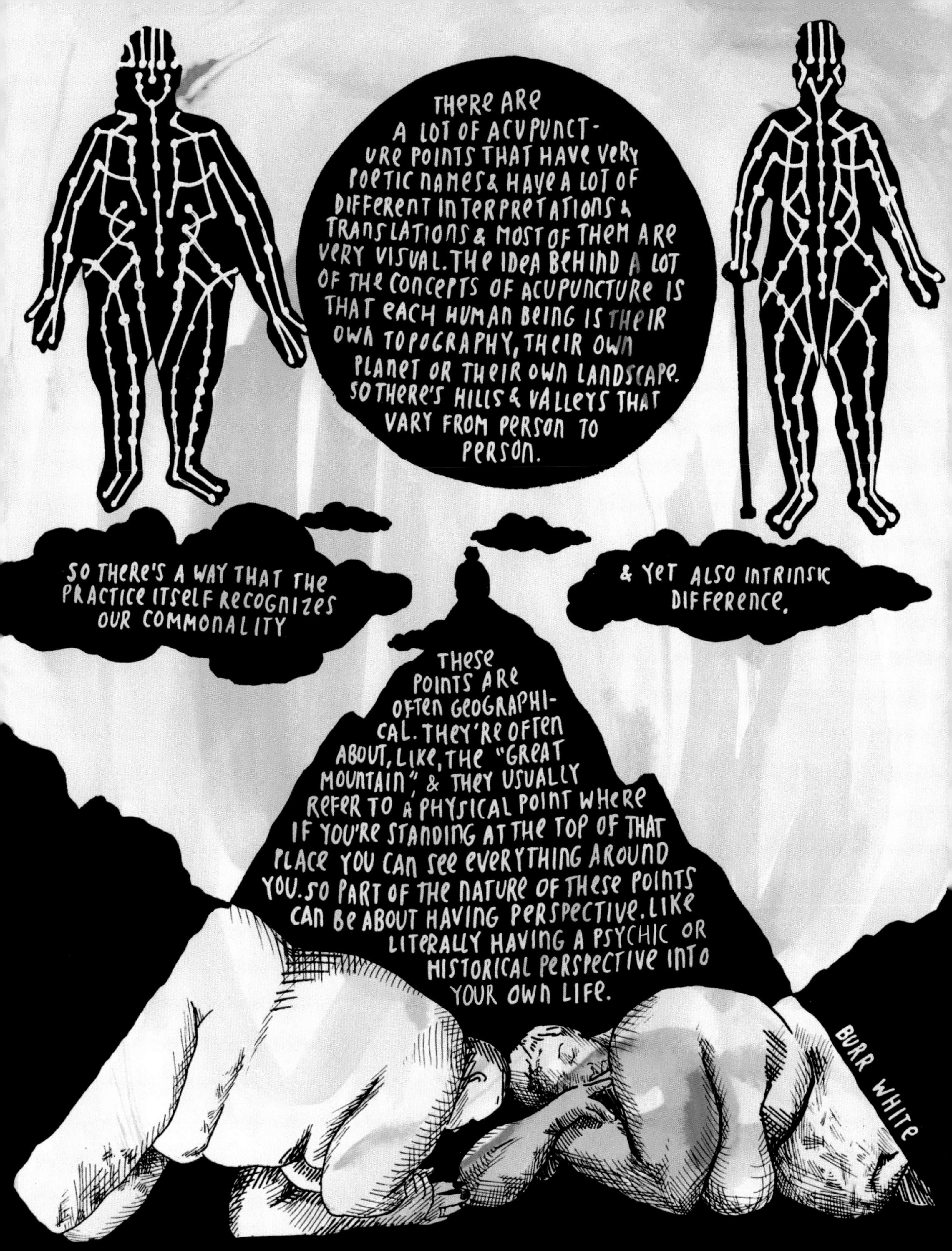
THERE ARE A LOT OF ACUPUNCT-URE POINTS THAT HAVE VERY POETIC NAMES & HAVE A LOT OF DIFFERENT INTERPRETATIONS & TRANSLATIONS & MOST OF THEM ARE VERY VISUAL. THE IDEA BEHIND A LOT OF THE CONCEPTS OF ACUPUNCTURE IS THAT EACH HUMAN BEING IS THEIR OWN TOPOGRAPHY, THEIR OWN PLANET OR THEIR OWN LANDSCAPE. SO THERE'S HILLS & VALLEYS THAT VARY FROM PERSON TO PERSON.
SO THERE'S A WAY THAT THE PRACTICE ITSELF RECOGNIZES OUR COMMONALITY
& YET ALSO INTRINSIC DIFFERENCE.
THESE POINTS ARE OFTEN GEOGRAPHI-CAL. THEY'RE OFTEN ABOUT, LIKE, THE "GREAT MOUNTAIN" & THEY USUALLY REFER TO A PHYSICAL POINT WHERE IF YOU'RE STANDING AT THE TOP OF THAT PLACE YOU CAN SEE EVERYTHING AROUND YOU. SO PART OF THE NATURE OF THESE POINTS CAN BE ABOUT HAVING PERSPECTIVE. LIKE LITERALLY HAVING A PSYCHIC OR HISTORICAL PERSPECTIVE INTO YOUR OWN LIFE.
BURR WHITE

FOR INSTANCE TO DEAL WITH PAIN, NOW YOU CAN LOOK AT IT & YOU COULDN'T BEFORE BUT YOU'VE REACHED THE TOP OF THAT PEAK & NOW YOU CAN SEE THE LANDSCAPE AROUND YOU.

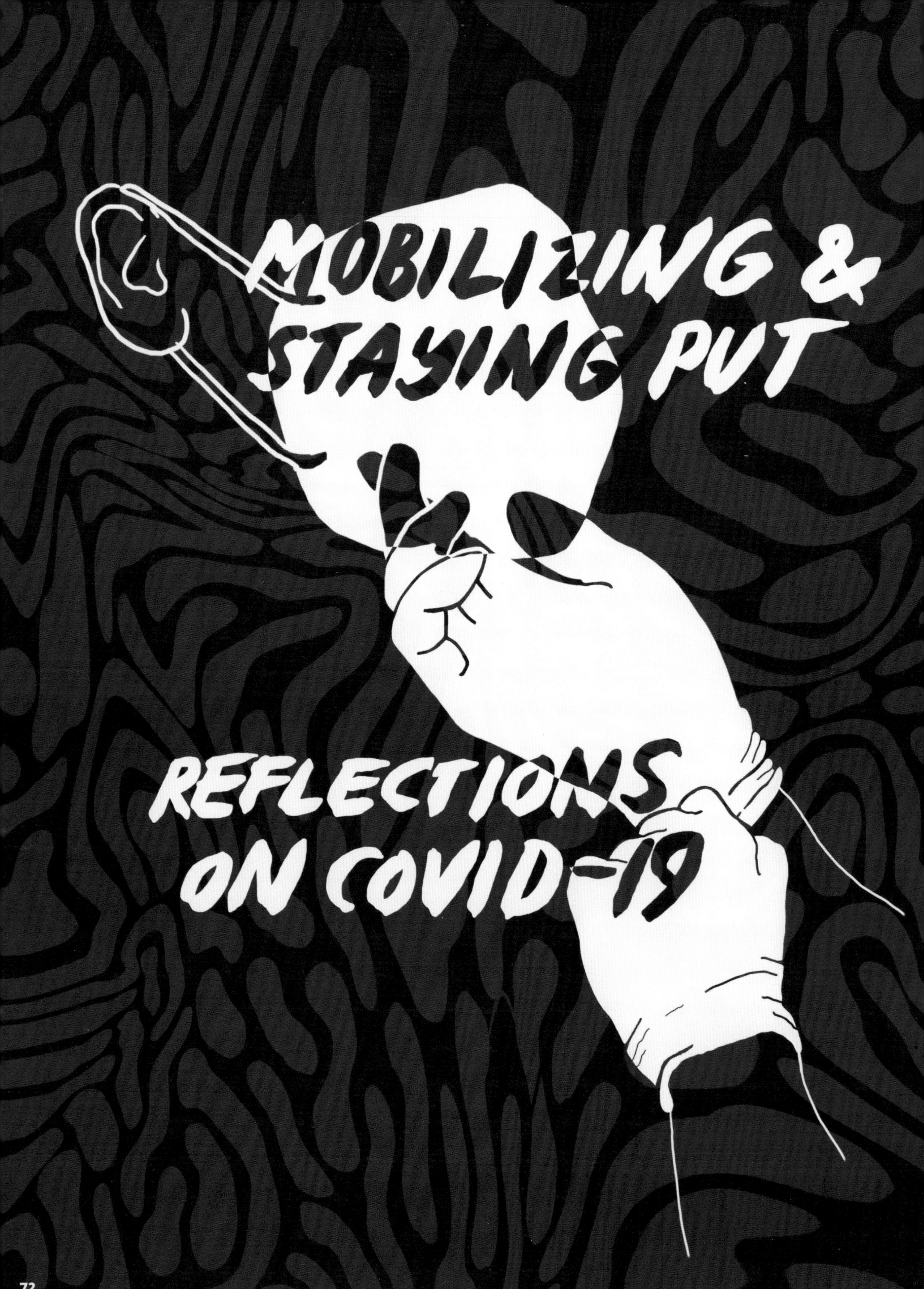
MOBILIZING &
STAYING PUT
REFLECTIONS
ON COVID-19

# A PRAISESONG FOR SICK BLK WIMMIN

BY RA MALIKA IMHOTEP

INSPIRED BY JOHANNA HEDVA'S "SICK WOMAN" THEORY

IN 1964, WHEN FANNIE LOU HAMER VENTURED UP SOUTH TO SHARE A HARLEM STAGE WITH MALCOLM X & SAID, "ALL MY LIFE I'VE BEEN SICK & TIRED. NOW I'M SICK & TIRED OF BEING SICK & TIRED," HER SICKNESS WAS NOT A METAPHOR.

IT WAS A REALITY, AN ACCESS ISSUE, THE WAY HER BODY BORE THE WEIGHT OF THE LABORS IT WAS ASKED TO PERFORM.

AFTER & WITH JUNE JORDAN'S ANGER + FLO KENNEDY'S FUSED SPINE + HARRIET TUBMAN'S HYPERSOMNIA + FANNIE LOU HAMER'S EXHAUSTION + AUDRE LORDE'S SACRED FEELING + OCTAVIA BUTLER'S KNOWING

"I AM JUST ONE OF THE PEOPLE WHO IS SICK OF THE SOCIAL ORDER, SICK OF THE ESTABLISHMENT, SICK TO MY SOUL OF IT ALL..." —NINA SIMONE

THE SICKNESS THAT COMES TO ME IS PERSISTENT YET AVOIDS DIAGNOSIS. WHEN I SCRAPE TOGETHER MY COINS TO GO TO THE DOCTOR I OFTEN LEAVE FEELING DISMISSED & STILL AILING. I HAVE A BLACK MAMA WHO IS QUICK TO TELL ME NOT TO CLAIM MY SICKNESS & I EMPATHIZE WITH HER DESIRE TO IMBUE ME WITH AN IMPENETRABLE SENSE OF RESILIENCE. MY BLACK MAMA WAS ONCE A BLACK GIRL WHO WOULD RESPOND TO NEGLECT WITH INTENSE BOUTS OF SICKNESS THAT REQUIRED HOSPITALIZATION. MY BLACK MAMA WAS ONCE A BLACK GIRL WHO INTERNALIZED NEGLECT & SPAT IT BACK OUT AS SICKNESS.

FANNIE LOU HAMER

RA MALIKA IMHOTEP

MY MAMA HAS DEDICATED HER LIFE TO WORKING TO ERADICATE HEALTH DISPARITIES AMONGST LOW INCOME BLACK COMMUNITIES IN ATLANTA.

MY MAMA IS OFTEN SICK & TIRED.

When the
pandemic hit, for a
moment black folks
entertained fantasies of
immunity but then our deaths
began to catch up with us
so suddenly. stay-at-home!
rest! grieve! produce!
heal! organize! how?
I think sick blk
wimmin have
been making
sense of this
for a long time.
sick as in ill, deviant,
perverse, excessive. blk as in
BLACK, of african descent & opaque.
wimmin as in collective, never singular & exceeding
+ subverting + rejecting binary conceptions of gender.

ntozake shange called it a "metaphysical dilemma." I think sick blk
wimmin—from mary jones, phillis wheatley, up to harriet tubman carried on by fannie lou hamer, &
further through flo kennedy, audre lorde, june jordan, miss major, & all the queer & deviant blk
wimmin + femmehoods we find home in— have been knowing something deep about this kind of
embattled survival. it also does not surprise me that a deep tradition of sick blk wimmin's
organizing & cultural work comes out of the south. I think a lot about
how being so close literally & figuratively to the plantations our ancestors
once stewarded marks us & shapes the way we move through the world. some say our
sickness is proof of the weather, or that the constant duress black folks have had
to make life out of has imprinted itself on to our nervous systems.

*image inspired by cover illustration of octavia butler's
"parable of the sower" by john jude palencar

When we talk about how southern black folks face alarming
"health disparities," we are saying that we are sick. and not sick
because there is something inherently wrong with us, but because
the world we've been given unto structurally & system—
ically disrupts our access to wellness.

I THINK WE SICK BLK WIMMIN CULTIVATE OUR "KNOW-HOW" FROM AN ACUTE AWARENESS OF OUR VULNERABILITIES.

WE AIN'T LEFT WITH MUCH CHOICE BUT TO GET FAMILIAR WITH THEM, TO LEARN TO OPEN OUR MOUTHS & NAME THEM ('CAUSE NOBODY ELSE WILL). THIS IS THE WORK OF EMBRACING VULNERABILITY'S CHARGE TO TAKE FULL CARE OF OURSELVES & EACH OTHER. IF VULNERABILITY IS THE BODY'S WAY OF RESPONDING TO SOCIAL, POLITICAL, & ENVIRONMENTAL INEQUITIES & DRAWING OUR ATTENTION TO ITS NEEDS,

IT COMES AS NO SURPRISE THAT THE MOST VULNERABLE ARE OFTEN THE MOST SKILLED STEWARDS & CARE TAKERS. AND IN OUR WHITE SUPREMACIST CAPITALIST CISHETEROPATRIARCHAL SOCIETY IT COMES AS NO SHOCK THAT THIS CARE WORK IS SEVERELY UNDERVALUED. BUT SICK BLK WIMMIN KNOW THE LABOR OF OUR LIVING IS SOMETHING INVALUABLE THAT CAPITALIST METRICS COULD NEVER HOLD.

BUT STILL, SOMEONE, SOMETHING, NEEDS TO HOLD US.

# A POEM FOR MY AMA

AFTER A YEAR OF HER PASSING
BY NUBE F. CRUZ

1.
I LOVED YOU MORE THAN THE SKY.
I LOVED YOU MORE THAN THE TREES AT FULL BLOOM & THE COPALLI
THAT SEEPS BLOOD RED THROUGH THE HUSKS OF MAIZE IN THE FALL

YOU ARE GONE AMA                    MY BIRTH GIVER
THE SKY ILLUMINATES MAYBE AS THEY TELL STORIES OF
WARRIOR WOMXN GIVING BIRTH IN MESOAMERICA OR
... APACHE WARRIOR WOMEN WHO LED
DIFFERENT REVOLTS

BEING NDN AND
MEXICAN WAS HARD

YOUR SWEAT, BLOOD, TEARS TAUGHT ME THAT

AS I LOOK AT THE LAND & SEE THE CRIMSON EROSIONS OF THIS
PANDEMIC I SEE HOW IT IS BETTER YOU ARE AN ANCESTOR NOW

AS I KNOW FOR SURE YOU WOULD'VE HATED SEEING ALL THIS DRAMA

YOU WERE SUCH A SHIT TALKER

WOULD TALK YOUR ASS OFF ABOUT THE NEIGHBORS BEING WASTEFUL & I CONTEMPLATE
IF THAT HAD TO DO WITH OUR WAY OF LIFE & OUR CONNECTION TO THE LAND OR IF IT
WAS JUST PART OF YOUR ANGER AT THE THINGS YOU HAD TO STRUGGLE THROUGH

I WONDER HOW MUCH JOY WAS A PART OF YOU

EVEN AT
THE END
OF IT

AND WHEN
YOU WEREN'T
LAUGHING

WHEN YOU HAD
TOO MANY
FEELINGS YOU
CUSSED PEOPLE OUT
& JUST GAVE THE LOOK

WHILE YOU WERE
STRUGGLING TO
SURVIVE

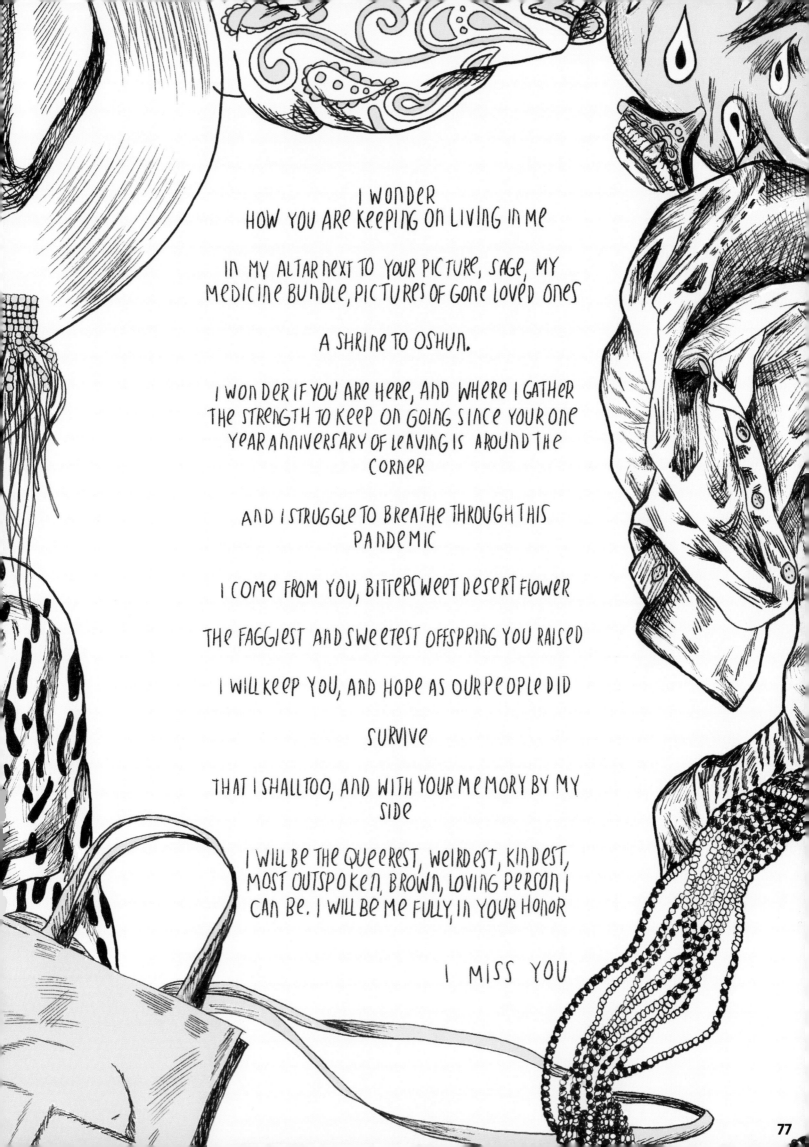

I WONDER
HOW YOU ARE KEEPING ON LIVING IN ME

IN MY ALTAR NEXT TO YOUR PICTURE, SAGE, MY
MEDICINE BUNDLE, PICTURES OF GONE LOVED ONES

A SHRINE TO OSHUN.

I WONDER IF YOU ARE HERE, AND WHERE I GATHER
THE STRENGTH TO KEEP ON GOING SINCE YOUR ONE
YEAR ANNIVERSARY OF LEAVING IS AROUND THE
CORNER

AND I STRUGGLE TO BREATHE THROUGH THIS
PANDEMIC

I COME FROM YOU, BITTERSWEET DESERT FLOWER

THE FAGGIEST AND SWEETEST OFFSPRING YOU RAISED

I WILL KEEP YOU, AND HOPE AS OUR PEOPLE DID

SURVIVE

THAT I SHALL TOO, AND WITH YOUR MEMORY BY MY
SIDE

I WILL BE THE QUEEREST, WEIRDEST, KINDEST,
MOST OUTSPOKEN, BROWN, LOVING PERSON I
CAN BE. I WILL BE ME FULLY, IN YOUR HONOR

I MISS YOU

2. AS WE MOVE FORWARD IN THESE TIMES ALL I CAN THINK OF HOW IS HOW INDIGENOUS PEOPLES HAVE SURVIVED MOST.

70 PERCENT OF OUR INDIGENOUS POPULATIONS ACROSS THE AMERICAS WERE GONE AFTER EUROPEANS LANDED

NUBE F. CRUZ

NATIVE PEOPLE LIVING IN INDIAN COUNTRY AND OUR BARRIOS ARE BEING AFFECTED

ANCESTRAL MEMORY RESIDES

OUR CONNECTION TO THE LAND AND OUR CONNECTION TO OUR HEALTH ARE TIED

IN THE MIDST OF THIS PANDEMIC I HOPE THAT WE REMEMBER

REMEMBER THOSE FALLEN

SAY THEIR NAMES OUT LOUD
SAY THEIR NAMES OUT LOUD
SAY THEIR NAMES OUT LOUD

NOW MORE THAN EVER WE NEED TO BURN OUR MEDICINES, PRAY, COLLECT OUR STORIES, USE OUR BUNDLES, PROVIDE AID TO OUR NATIONS AS BEST WE CAN.

FROM ACJACHEMEN AND TONGVA LAND
TO OHLONE LANDS.
LEARN THE HISTORIES OF THE PEOPLES'
LANDS YOU RESIDE IN.

PRAY, FIGHT, REMEMBER.
PRAY, FIGHT, REMEMBER.
PRAY, FIGHT, REMEMBER.

HEAL.

THIS PIECE IS
NOT POSSIBLE WITHOUT
THE NATIVE AND XICANA
WOMEN AND TWO SPIRITS IN
MY LIFE

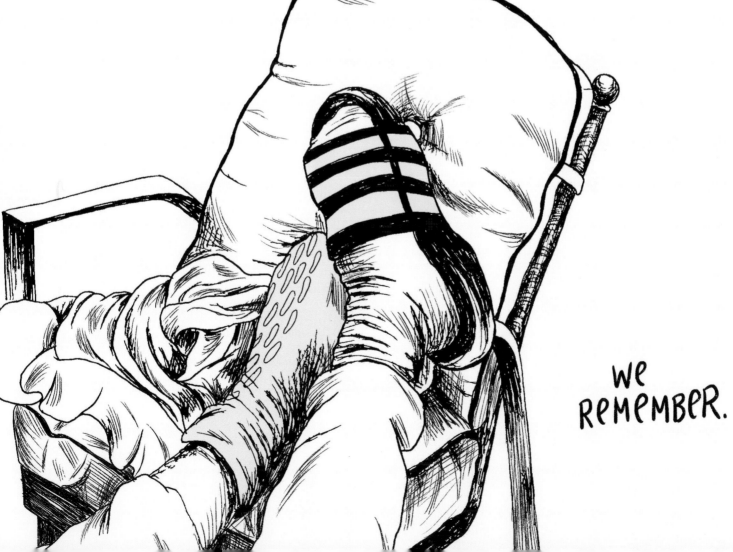

WE
REMEMBER.

# TO THOSE WHO KEEP SHOWING UP?

## MUTUAL AID ORGANIZING IN RURAL SPACE & PLACE

### BY BRENDA ANGELICA GUTIERREZ MORA

THE SAN JOAQUIN VALLEY (SJV) IN CALIFORNIA HIGHLIGHTS THE INTERSECTIONS OF SYSTEMS THAT HARM THE MOST VULNERABLE COMMUNITY MEMBERS. AT PLAY ARE ENVIRONMENTAL RACISM, ECONOMIC INEQUALITY & LABOR EXPLOITATION, OBSTACLES TO EDUCATIONAL ATTAINMENT, & THE CRIMINALIZATION OF COMMUNITIES OF COLOR. MORE THAN A QUARTER MILLION WORKERS ARE NONCITIZENS, WITH AN ESTIMATED 112,034 IMMIGRANTS BEING UNDOCUMENTED.[1]

DESPITE BEING THE BREADBASKET OF THE COUNTRY, MANY VALLEY WORKERS EXPERIENCE CONSISTENT & SEVERE HOUSING & FOOD INSECURITY.[2] THE BROADER CENTRAL CALIFORNIA LANDSCAPE, KNOWN AS THE CENTRAL VALLEY, IS HOME TO HALF OF CALIFORNIA'S STATE & FEDERAL CORRECTIONAL FACILITIES & ONE DETENTION CENTER, & HAS BEEN DUBBED PRISON ALLEY.[3]

AS A QUEER & NONBINARY LATINX BORN & RAISED IN THE SJV FROM A MIXED STATUS FAMILY, I KNOW HOW INCREDIBLY POWERFUL, BRILLIANT, & RESOURCEFUL OUR COMMUNITIES ARE, DESPITE OUR CONTEXT.

IN MARCH 2020, COVID-19 DISRUPTIONS CAUSED FOLKS TO GATHER & STRATEGIZE TO SUPPORT THE CENTRAL VALLEY COMMUNITY. THREE CRITICAL NEEDS WERE IDENTIFIED: BASIC NEEDS SECURITY, POLICY DEMANDS FOR ROBUST PROTECTIONS, & CREATING A NEW FUND. THE COLLECTIVE THAT GREW AROUND THESE EFFORTS IS NOW THE CENTRAL VALLEY MUTUAL AID & COLLECTIVE CARE NETWORK (CV MAN).

AS ORGANIZERS, WE TAPPED INTO OUR NETWORKS TO BETTER UNDERSTAND HOW TO SUPPORT THE FOLKS MOST IMPACTED BY THE PANDEMIC, WHO WERE ALREADY MADE VULNERABLE BY LIVING & EXPERIENCING A CONVERGENCE OF THE INDUSTRIAL COMPLEXES IN RURAL CALIFORNIA: THE PRISON INDUSTRIAL COMPLEX, THE NONPROFIT INDUSTRIAL COMPLEX, THE MEDICAL INDUSTRIAL COMPLEX, & THE MILITARY INDUSTRIAL COMPLEX.

[1] OROZCO FLORES, E., & PADILLA, A. (2020). "NON-CITIZEN WORKERS IN THE SAN JOAQUIN VALLEY." POLICY BRIEF. UNIVERSITY OF CALIFORNIA MERCED.
[2] OROZCO FLORES, E., & PADILLA, A. (2020). "RENT BURDEN AMONG CALIFORNIA WORKER HOUSEHOLDS," RESEARCH BRIEF. UNIVERSITY OF CALIFORNIA MERCED.
[3] BRAZ, R., & GILMORE, C. (2006). "JOINING FORCES: PRISONS & ENVIRONMENTAL JUSTICE IN RECENT CALIFORNIA ORGANIZING." RADICAL HISTORY REVIEW 96. MARHO

JASMINE LEIVA

CRISANTEMA GALLARDO

BRENDA ANGELICA GUTIERREZ MORA

MONICA GOMEZ

NOT PORTRAYED:
JOODY MARKS

LAUREN ARNEST

DESMARIE JACKSON

AS A CO-FOUNDER OF CVMAN, IT WAS IMPORTANT TO ME THAT OUR RESPONSE BE ROOTED IN COLLECTIVE CARE & CARE WORK, LIBERATORY ACCESS, INTERDEPENDENCE, AND ACCESS INTIMACY, ESPECIALLY DURING TIMES CALLING FOR SOCIAL DISTANCING. WE MET WITH COMMUNITY-BASED GROUPS THAT CENTER CARE TO BUILD ON EXISTING KNOWLEDGE. I FEEL GRATEFUL TO BE IN COMMUNITY WITH QUEER SIBLINGS LOCALLY & NATIONWIDE THROUGH NETWORKS ONLINE & IN PERSON WHICH HAVE ALLOWED ME TO BUILD POWER COAST TO COAST AND ACROSS BORDERS, INCLUDING THE RIDGEWOOD MUTUAL AID NETWORK & NORCAL RESIST, A POWERFUL ORGANIZATION BASED IN CALIFORNIA WHO HAS SUPPORTED OUR WORK BY TAKING US UNDER THEIR WING.

THOSE WHO HAVE KEPT SHOWING UP UNDERSTAND THE COMMITMENT OF DEEP SOLIDARITY, THE COMMITMENT TO BETRAY OUR PRIVILEGE, & THE COMMITMENT OF BLACK & INDIGENOUS LIBERATION. BUILDING AN INTERGENERATIONAL COLLECTIVE OVER EIGHT COUNTIES WAS POSSIBLE BY ENSURING A BOTTOM-UP APPROACH TO CONNECT FOLKS TO A CENTRALIZED HUB OF SHARED VALUES & A CRITICAL FRAMEWORK ROOTED IN BLACK & INDIGENOUS TRADITION.

KASSANDRA HISHIDA

CLAUDIA CRISTEL CORTES

SERVIN JENSEN

MARINARDE SOTO

WILLIAM KELLY

TANISHA MCCLAIN

GRISANTI AVENDAÑO

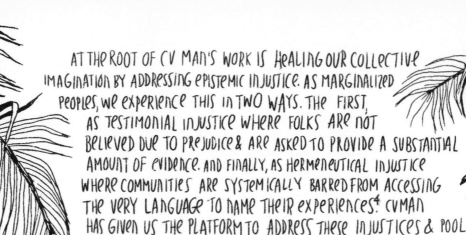

AT THE ROOT OF CV MAN'S WORK IS HEALING OUR COLLECTIVE IMAGINATION BY ADDRESSING EPISTEMIC INJUSTICE. AS MARGINALIZED PEOPLES, WE EXPERIENCE THIS IN TWO WAYS. THE FIRST, AS TESTIMONIAL INJUSTICE WHERE FOLKS ARE NOT BELIEVED DUE TO PREJUDICE & ARE ASKED TO PROVIDE A SUBSTANTIAL AMOUNT OF EVIDENCE. AND FINALLY, AS HERMENEUTICAL INJUSTICE WHERE COMMUNITIES ARE SYSTEMICALLY BARRED FROM ACCESSING THE VERY LANGUAGE TO NAME THEIR EXPERIENCES.[4] CVMAN HAS GIVEN US THE PLATFORM TO ADDRESS THESE INJUSTICES & POOL OUR RESOURCES & WORK TOWARD HEALING JUSTICE, ABOLITION, WORKER-OWNED COOPERATIVES, & MUTUAL AID.

AT THE TIME OF WRITING IN JUNE 2020, WE HAVE FUNDRAISED OVER 1.2 MILLION DOLLARS AND ARE INTENTIONAL ABOUT

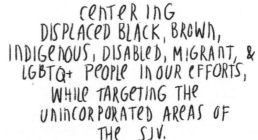

CENTERING DISPLACED BLACK, BROWN, INDIGENOUS, DISABLED, MIGRANT, & LGBTQ+ PEOPLE IN OUR EFFORTS, WHILE TARGETING THE UNINCORPORATED AREAS OF THE SJV.

ALTHOUGH THIS STARTED AS COVID-19 RELIEF, WE'RE GEARING UP TO CONTINUE SUPPORTING DIRECTLY IMPACTED PEOPLE IN THE SJV, PARTICULARLY AS THE STATE & LOCAL GOVERNMENTS REOPEN DESPITE HEALTH CONCERNS, TO CONTINUE BUILDING POWER & RESILIENCE. THIS WORK HAS BEEN MOVED ALONG BY THE ENDLESS LOVE, CARE, & LABOR OF QUEER, TRANS & GENDER-NONCONFORMING PEOPLE OF COLOR. WE ORGANIZE FOR OUR SURVIVAL, FOR OUR LIVELIHOOD, & THE LIVELIHOOD OF OUR FAMILIES, BOTH BIOLOGICAL & CHOSEN. WE BREATHE LIFE INTO EACH OTHER, WE HOLD EACH OTHER, WE BELIEVE THAT WE WILL WIN. OUR WORK IS EVERYWHERE.

[4] FRICKER, M. "EPISTEMIC INJUSTICE: POWER AND THE ETHICS OF KNOWING." OXFORD: OXFORD UNIVERSITY PRESS, 2007.

# ACKNOWLEDGMENTS

Thank you to all the contributors, who shared their experiences, passion, and vulnerability with me. I so deeply appreciate the opportunity to learn from all of you and your lived brilliance.

To every friend, love, and comrade who transcribed an interview for this, who recommended participants, who read my zines, who talked me through my process, who weighed in on an idea. We need support networks to thrive emotionally, creatively, and spiritually, and I am so grateful for the queer people in my life who've played many different roles in my growth as an artist and a person. Thank you for the feedback, the compassion, the challenges, the insights, the care.

To Artist Trust, which awarded me a grant to start this project when it was just an idea blossoming in my head in 2016. To anyone who advocates for, or participates in, the redistribution of wealth on an individual or systemic level.

To Leah, for mentoring me (and many others!) through the publication process. Thank you for helping people grow their work from sprouted seeds to sturdy trees.

To Brian Lam and the entire Arsenal Pulp team. You believed in my vision and trusted me to carry this project out into a physical embodiment of my creative dreams. Thank you so much for allowing me to be a part of the decision-making process and encouraging my creative autonomy.

To my mom, Liz Liao, and my bestie, Liv, for years (decades) of genuine encouragement and thoughtful engagement. I am an artist who believes in herself because of you.

# CONTRIBUTOR BIOGRAPHIES

**SZE-YANG ADE-LAM** is a queer, Asian, nonbinary storyteller and community developer via dance, kung fu, words, drawings, film, and photo. Sze-Yang shares stories for love, liberation, representation, and empowerment, as an independent artist and as part of ILL NANA/DiverseCity Dance Company. Since 2011, Sze-Yang has created more accessible and affirming dance education and performance opportunities for QTBIPOCs and their adjacent communities, as well as advocated for change in the arts. Find Sze-Yang on Instagram *@seeyinandyang*.

**NICOLE ARTEAGA** (she/her) is a mixed race, queer, fat, cis femme. For the past eight years, QTPOC organizing, public education, and reproductive justice have been her political home. Nicole works to fund abortion and build power with the National Network of Abortion Funds and fills her free time with ceramics and baking for her loved ones. Originally from the Midwest, she has familial roots in Mexico and lives on traditional Tonkawa land (Austin, Texas) with her partner and two pets. She's a deep feeler and good eater.

**JULES BALDINO** is a nonbinary Aries femme living in unceded Tohono O'odham territory. Fight for Black lives, fuck all cops, build new worlds is our imperative, with Black and Indigenous communities as our leadership. Smooches.

**NUBE F. CRUZ** is a Yaqui/Mixteco and Xicanx writer, lover of fashion, Indigenous lands rights activist, survivor advocate, artist, and cultural worker. They work with tribal communities in Southern California and migrant communities in Los Angeles. They are starting to write and work in their art practice again. You can follow them on Instagram *@XXNUBEXX*.

**CEYENNE DOROSHOW** (pronounced *Kai-Ann*) is a compassionate powerhouse performer, activist, organizer, community-based researcher, and public figure in the trans and sex worker rights movements. As the founder and executive director of G.L.I.T.S., she works to provide holistic care to LGBTQ sex workers while serving on the following boards: SWOP-USA, Caribbean Equality Project, SOAR Institute, and NYTAG. As an international public speaker, she presents at the Desiree Alliance, the Creating Change Conference, SisterSong, Harm Reduction Coalition, and the International AIDS Conference. She was a featured emcee for Toronto Pride and MoMA/PS1's Sex Workers' Festival of Resistance, lifting her voice as a trans woman of color. Ceyenne has featured heavily in the media, performing on television in Showtime's *Oz* and the documentaries *The Red Umbrella Diaries* and *MAJOR!*. Known for her skills in the kitchen, Ceyenne co-authored the Caribbean cookbook *Cooking in Heels*, while incarcerated on prostitution charges. She is currently working on her second book, *Falling into the Fire*.

**GELENI FONTAINE** is a fat, queer and trans, disabled, nonbinary Latinx person raised and thriving in Brooklyn, New York. As an acupuncturist, East Asian medicine healer, and registered nurse, they use knowledge of Western allopathic medicine to support their holistic East Asian practice, helping individuals navigate both health care systems. As a disabled healer with chronic pain and illness, they are devoted to working with all their communities from within their intersections. Their goal is to empower individuals and nourish healing toward a more just and loving world for us all.

**RYAN GILBERT** (a.k.a. phlegm) is a New Orleans native visual artist taking African religious and ceremonial face paint and reimagining it in a modern context. His work (and by extension his life) makes a production about the necessity and value of Black spiritual presence. It serves to more firmly connect his Black spiritual concept of time: connecting the past to the present and the present to the future. Communally sacred. Personally precious.

**MIRNA HAIDAR** is a Juris Doctor, and they identify as a queer Muslim immigrant mama activist. She worked and organized around LGBTQ rights, migrant workers' rights, and climate change in Lebanon and the United States. They love to have conversations about imagining a world with no incarceration, no borders, no military, and, of course, no police. Their work is centered on practicing accountability without disposability.

**RA MALIKA IMHOTEP** is a Black feminist writer and performance artist from Atlanta, Georgia. As a scholar and cultural worker, Ra is invested in exploring relationships between queerness, Black femininity, Southern vernacular culture, and the performance of labor. Ra is a co-convener, with Miyuki Baker, of the embodied spiritual-political education project the Church of Black Feminist Thought. More info on Ra's work can be found at *blackfeministstudy.org.*

**PHOS IVESTEI** is a queer, nonbinary creature from the Virginia swamps who has worked in many different intersections of the LGBTQ+ community. They strive to maintain and practice trauma-informed assistance for persons seeking to legally change their identity documents to reflect their true name and gender. They, with a team of other trans and gender-nonconforming folks, created a state-by-state database of laws and processes related to legal name and gender marker changes as a public resource. Today, they continue this work, in addition to legal work in discrimination against LGBTQ+ people and local/state laws that affect the community in Pennsylvania.

**ANABEL KHOO** is a holistic mental health counselor, artist, writer, and facilitator dedicated to building capacity and support for collective healing. She works through an embodied, relational, and visionary politics of liberation, engaging with lived experience to uplift and harvest collective wisdom and skills to create a better world.

**AMBER KIM** is an activist, witch, nerd, and trans woman who believes in comforting the disturbed and disturbing the comfortable. She is currently incarcerated in Washington State. To learn more about Amber, check out *AmberFayefoxKim.WordPress.com* or contact her on *JPay.com.*

**DUSTY LAMAY** ponders over stars, patterns, futures, pasts, presence, and possibilities. He works with the stars and in the legal field. He is an Okie who has spent nearly half his life in California or the Pacific Northwest, where he currently lives. Astrology consultations for new clients are sometimes available. You can reach Dusty about astrology at *nightbirdastrology@gmail.com.*

**CALEB LUNA** is a fat, queer (of color) critical theorist, artist, and performance scholar. As a PhD candidate in performance studies at UC Berkeley, they research performances of eating and historicizing cultural representations of fat embodiment within the ongoing settler colonization of North America. As an activist political thinker, they are interested in engaging embodied difference as a generative resource toward fatter understandings of collective freedom.

**BRENDA ANGELICA GUTIÉRREZ MORA** is a fat, queer, nonbinary, and disabled poet and performer, writer, artist, organizer, and cultural strategist of color born and raised in occupied Yokuts land (so-called San Joaquin Valley in the heart of California). They invite folks into their big, bold dreams of collective care, collective liberation, harm reduction, and interdependence with a clear commitment to Black liberation and Indigenous sovereignty. What we build is as important as how we build it. They ask, "What will you build (or destroy) for your next seven generations?"

**STEPH NIAUPARI** (they/elle) is an Ecuadorian PapiFemme. Raised on bacon, egg, and cheese sandwiches in Queens, New York, Steph has found their home and community within Washington, DC. As the founder of Plantita Power, Steph bridges communities by centering language justice in the garden and providing access to QTBIPOC folks interested in growing their own food. Most recently, Steph and their team launched a QTBIPOC seedling program expanding to nine states, which distributes free monthly plants via local deliveries or mail. With each plant, they all hope community healing can become a little bit easier.

**CYD NOVA** lives in Brooklyn, New York, with his partner, his four roommates, and his dog, Farrah. He's a writer, an enthusiastic home cook, and a consultant with Trans Equity Consulting.

**LEAH LAKSHMI PIEPZNA-SAMARASINHA** is a queer disabled femme writer and performer of Burgher/Tamil Sri Lankan and Irish/Roma ascent. Her most recent titles are the nonfiction book *Care Work: Dreaming Disability Justice*, the poetry book *Tonguebreaker*, and the co-edited nonfiction anthology *Beyond Survival: Strategies and Stories from the Transformative Justice Movement* (with Ejeris Dixon). Her memoir *Dirty River* was a finalist for a Lambda Literary Award and a Publishing Triangle Award (Judy Grahn Award for Lesbian Nonfiction). She is also the author of the poetry books *Bodymap* and *Love Cake* (Lambda Literary Award winner) and *Consensual Genocide*, and the co-editor of *The Revolution Starts at Home: Confronting Intimate Violence in Activist Communities*. She is the co-founder of Mangos with Chili, North America's touring queer and trans people of color cabaret, and a lead artist with the disability justice incubator Sins Invalid.

**JAYE SABLAN** is an Indigenous Chamoru poet and writer from the Pacific island of Saipan in the Mariana Islands archipelago. Her work is in *Nepantla*, *Yellow Medicine Review*, *As/Us*, and *Bitch*. Jaye's poetry has also been featured in the illustrations, film, and art exhibitions of queer and trans visual artists based in the U.S. Pacific Northwest and beyond. She lives and works in Seattle—the unceded ancestral homelands of the People of the Inside, dxʷdəwʔabš (Duwamish), who continue to steward their lands and waters to this day.

**TIFFANY ST. BUNNY** is the co-founder of Trans Assistance Project and operations director at Trans Lifeline. Her hobbies include riding her bike really far, taking beautiful photos, and exploring the outdoors with her dog, Lu. One of these days she hopes to publish a print copy of her photography project "Trucksluts Magazine," but in the meantime, she's content to off-road in the desert and find secret swimming holes in the mountains. She's adamant that the best movie ever made is *Tremors*.

**STELLA SHAFFER** is a founding member of the Trans Assistance Project, which is now a part of the grassroots hotline and microgrant organization Trans Lifeline. Stella is passionate about nonprofit work and building social systems that better serve trans people.

**RAVEN TAYLOR** is an emerging writer based in Seattle, Washington.

**VIVI VERONICA** is a West Coast baby trying to tap into the energetic nodes of the changing world to focus on our landscapes of spirituality and the deep complexities of human interaction. Her goals and life work are related to mental health, drug use, our relationship to order and chaos, autonomy/liberation, and figuring out ways to successfully care for and love each other. She uses writing as a medium to process the inherently absurd and beautiful ways these topics play out in our lives.

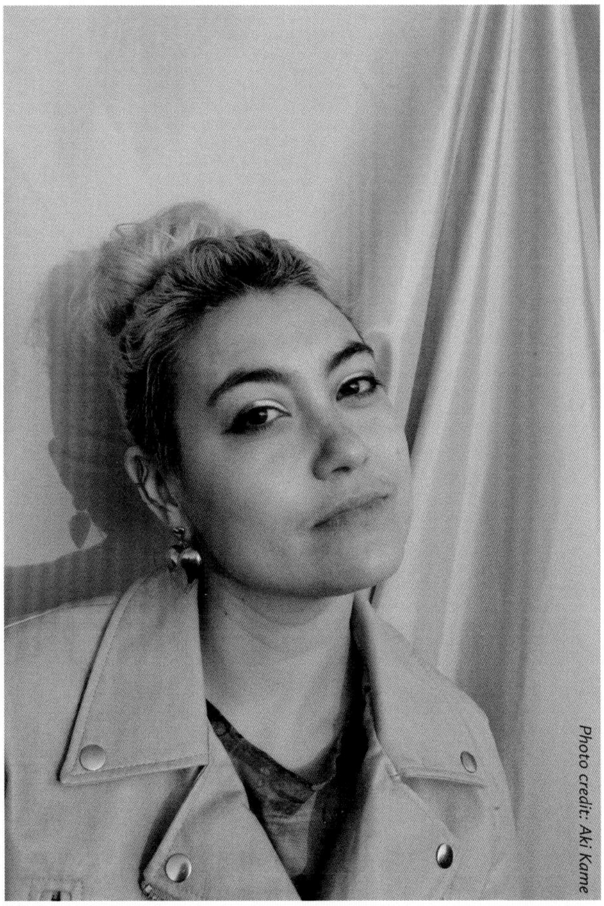
Photo credit: Aki Kame

**SYAN ROSE** (pronounced *Sy-Ann*) is an illustrator and comic artist whose work plays with both surrealist and representational imagery to approach topics of personal history, politics, accountability, and healing. She's been published in *Bitch*, *Slate*, *Gay Magazine*, *Truthout*, and *Autostraddle*, and has self-produced many comics and zines.
*syanrose.com*